FORCES TO BE RECKONED WITH

Formidable Men

Jewel Hampton

FORCES TO BE RECKONED WITH: FORMIDABLE MEN

Copyright © 2023 Jewel Hampton

All rights reserved. No part of this book may be reproduced or transmitted in any form or by any means without written permission from the author.

ISBN: 979-8-9891228-0-6

Printed in the USA

All Scripture quotations are taken from the King James Bible Version

Cover design: Jewel Hampton

Photos licensed from Shutterstock

DEDICATION

This book is dedicated to my father, whom I miss every day, to my grandfathers, brothers, uncles, grandsons, nephews, and cousins. It is dedicated to the pastors, ministers, and teachers who have contributed to my spiritual growth and edification. Men among men. Thank you so very much.

This book is also for those men everywhere who need guidance and inspiration; it is hoped the stories of the formidable men in this book who made such substantial contributions to Bible history will help you and strengthen you in your walk with Christ. May God bless you in a very special manner.

CONTENTS

YAHSHUA

1.	Adam	1
2.	Noah	6
3	Enoch	11
4.	Abraham 07 - 24	13
5.	Isaac	17
6.	Jacob	21
7.	Joseph	28
8.	Judah	31
9.	Moses	37
10.	Aaron	46
11.	Joshua	53
12.	Caleb	57
13.	Samson	62
14.	Samuel	69
15.	David	75
16.	Elijah	86
17.	Jonadab	100
18.	Job	106

19.	Daniel	120
20.	The Three Hebrew Boys	140
21.	Zacharias	145
22.	Josph of Nazareth	151
23.	Simeon	155
24.	John the Baptist	160
25.	The Apostles	166
26.	Nicodemus	176
27.	The Nobleman	182
28.	The Roman Centurion	184
29.	Jairus	189
30.	Zacchaeus	193
31.	Stephen	196
32.	Philip	201
33	Paul	206
Anonymous		224
A Few More Formidable Men		226

YAHSHUA

For when we were yet without strength, in due time Christ died for the ungodly. (Romans 5:6)

God, by his Divine Right and for his glory, created the universe and all that he wanted to be in it. Among the created, there is a distinct and perfect order for the creation. Adam was the first of his kind, and from him, all of mankind sprang. But even as all of mankind came through Adam, all sinned in him as the federal head of the family. Sin entered the world through Adam, the Law came through Moses, but grace, mercy, and peace came through YAHshua HaMashiach (Jesus the Messiah).

From Genesis through Revelation, the Bible is the story of Christ, his virgin birth, his teachings, the miracles he performed, his substitutionary death, and his resurrection.

And there are also many other things which Jesus did, the which, if they should be written every one, I suppose that even the world itself could not contain the books that should be written. Amen. (John 21:25V)

The Old Testament foretells, foreshadows, and typifies him. He appears in the Old Testament as the angel of the Lord. In the New Testament, he is revealed, he is the realization of the shadows, and he is the Great Antitype of all types of him. The reconciliation of mankind back to the Father came through Christ, our Savior. God used man to begin mankind, and he used himself wrapped in the form of a man to save it.

God has never left himself without a righteous man. When he would have destroyed all of mankind, Noah was found righteous before him. When Elijah thought he was the only one, God informed him, "I have left me seven thousand in Israel, all the knees which have not bowed unto Baal, and every mouth which hath not kissed him" (1 Kings 19:18).

We thank God that there are still righteous men standing on the only firm foundation, God's immutable, unperishable Word.

1 ADAM

And the LORD God formed man of the dust of the ground, and breathed into his nostrils the breath of life; and man became a living soul. (Genesis 2:7)

Adam, by the Divine Right of God, has an incomparable place in Scripture and the history of the universe: He was the first of humankind. "And God said, Let us make man in our image, after our likeness: and let them have dominion . . .." (Genesis 1:26). The "us" in making man "in our image" indicates the presence of what is called the Godhead: God the Father, God the Son, and God the Holy Spirit. Adam was the first of his kind, the first man, the first human, the first husband, and the first father. He is the only man to have another human taken out of him and the first man to succumb to temptation. He is the father of all living, the federal head of the human family. All mankind and womankind can trace themselves back to Adam.

"And the LORD God formed man of the dust of the ground, and breathed into his nostrils the breath of life; and man became a living soul" (Genesis 2:7). Adam was formed from the soil of the ground. The Hebrew word for man is "adam," and the word for soil or ground is "adamah." Adam is the only man ever to have known perfection, as temporary as it was. God created the Garden of Eden, a perfect paradise, and placed Adam in it to live and tend to it. Adam was free to eat everything the garden produced except the tree of knowledge of good and evil, "for in the day that thou eatest thereof thou shalt surely die" (Genesis 2:17).

God caused a deep sleep to come upon Adam, took one of his ribs from his side, and formed a mate to share his life, bear children, and enjoy Paradise. Adam first called her "woman."

> And Adam said, This is now bone of my bones, and flesh of my flesh: she shall be called Woman, because she was taken out of Man. Therefore shall a man leave his father and his mother, and shall cleave unto his wife: and they shall be one flesh. (Genesis 2:23-24)

Adam was given dominion over all other creations, and he named them.

> And out of the ground the LORD God formed every beast of the field, and every fowl of the air; and brought them unto Adam to see what he would call them: and whatsoever Adam called every living creature, that was the name thereof. (Genesis 2:19)

All was well with Adam and Eve. Everything was going according to God's perfect order until the day they disobeyed his commandment. Satan convinced Eve to eat of the tree of the knowledge of good and evil, and she gave some of the forbidden fruit to Adam, who was with her. They had been warned of the recompense of sinning against God, and it was immediate. The moment they disobeyed, they began to die. They had been created in the perfect image of God. Sin now marred that image. At that very moment, they became corruptible beings, and all mankind with them.

> Wherefore, as by one man sin entered into the world, and death by sin; and so death passed upon all men, for that all have sinned. (Romans 5:12).

Because all of mankind was within Adam and Eve, all mankind died with them. But God, in his great mercy, promised that through the very seed of the woman would one day come one that would utterly destroy the enemy. "And I will put enmity between thee and the woman, and between thy seed and her seed; it shall bruise thy head, and thou shalt bruise his heel" (Genesis 3:15).

The first couple were banished from Paradise. Cherubims and a flaming sword were placed at the east of the Garden of Eden to guard the Tree of Life, so they could not eat of it and live. They were dismissed with only the coverings given to them by the Lord to begin a new state of being. Adam now called his wife "Eve" because she was "the mother of all living."

An animal died so that our foreparents might be clothed. It was the first sacrifice. A sacrifice is a method of atoning for man's sins, but the blood of animals could never suffice as a permanent solution for cleansing humans of sin. The only solution was for God himself to take on the form of human flesh and shed the only perfect blood as a final sacrifice for sin.

Shammed by Satan, having lost immortality, and their relationship with God corrupted, Adam and Eve, are now driven from the only home they had known, the safety and familiarity of Paradise.

Together they had shared what no other humans would ever know; now Adam would become the first to know what it was to work all day in the ground from whence he came, and Eve would know what it was to suffer in childbearing. Yet the hope of redemption by the seed of the woman, the hope of a redeemer to save them from their sins and restore what had been lost, must have reigned with them for the rest of their lives.

Paul said, "And so it is written, The first man Adam was made a living soul; the last Adam was made a quickening spirit" (1 Corinthians 15:45).

Nevertheless death reigned from Adam to Moses, even over them that had not sinned after the similitude of Adam's transgression, who is the figure of him that was to come. (Romans 5:14)

Adam was a figure, a type, a pattern, a shadow, or a resemblance of him who was to come, YAHshua HaMashiach (Jesus The Messiah). He was the first shadow of the restoration to come. Through Adam, all mankind sinned and died, but life was restored through Christ.

But not as the offence, so also is the free gift. For if through the offence of one many be dead, much more the grace of God, and the gift by grace, which is by one man, Jesus Christ, hath abounded unto many And not as it was by one that sinned, so is the gift: for the judgment was by one to condemnation, but the free gift is of many offences unto justification. (Romans 5:15-16.)

All the days of Adam's life, he looked for the one to come and lived the rest of his accordingly. He passed down the hope of the Messiah. He was a force to be reckoned with, a formidable man.

2 NOAH

These are the generations of Noah: Noah was a just man and perfect in his generations, and Noah walked with God. (Genesis 6:9)

Noah had a great witness. God looked at the world and repented of having created it. But for one man, he would have destroyed "both man, and beast, and the creeping thing, and the fowls of the air" from the face of the earth (Genesis 6:7). "But Noah found grace in the eyes of the LORD" (Genesis 6:8).

In a cold and cruel world, where every man walked according to his own understanding, Noah only was found to walk with God. He was found upright, full of integrity by God. And so, when judgment was rendered for all of mankind, Noah and his family were saved from utter destruction. Noah had three sons: Shem, Ham, and Japheth (Genesis 6:10). Noah, his wife, sons, and their wives were spared to multiply and fill the land. Will God save the world for one righteous man? Yes. Stay righteous. God is seeking such men as you.

Noah was told to build an ark, which he built to the specific measurements God commanded (Genesis 6:14-16). "Thus did Noah; according to all that God commanded him, so did he" (Genesis 6:22).

Noah building an ark could not have been popular among people who had not seen storms or floods. Others may have even ridiculed him. A man of faith has no time to listen to the naysayers. He is too busy listening to the voice of God and obeying his commands. He walks in his integrity.

The ark would safely shelter Noah and his family during the catastrophic flood God would send upon the earth. Know that God will keep a righteous man in the time of storm. When all the world is shaking from strong winds, the man of God will stay on the ark and be saved. "But with thee will I establish my covenant; and thou shalt come into the ark, thou, and thy sons, and thy wife, and thy sons' wives with thee" (Genesis 6:18-21). Some scholars have compared the ark to the Tabernacle in the Wilderness, where the Spirit of God abided among his people in the Ark of the Covenant.

Noah not only saved humanity, but his act saved the beasts God created. He took seven pairs of every clean animal (those suitable for sacrifice), male and female, two of the animals considered unclean, male and female, and seven pairs of the birds that flew, male and female.

Noah and his family entered the ark with the animals when he was 600 years old, and after seven days, the rain began to pour. Know that age is of no importance to God using an individual. "In the six hundredth year of Noah's life, in the second month, the seventeenth day of the month, the same day were all the fountains of the great deep broken up, and the windows of heaven were opened" (Genesis 7:11).

For forty days and forty nights, the rain poured down. Everyone upon the face of the earth that was not in the ark was destroyed. The rains covered the treetops and the mountains until the ark floated above the earth. The waters stayed upon the earth for 150 days (Genesis 7:24). But Noah and his family were dry in the safety of God's ark. There is no storm that God cannot keep you in the midst of, no suffering that he is not with you. You are safe from the storms of life in the ark.

> And God remembered Noah, and every living thing, and all the cattle that was with him in the ark: and God made a wind to pass over the earth, and the waters asswaged. (Genesis 8:1)

God always remembers his people, and he remembered Noah. The rain ceased at the end of the 40 days. God caused a wind to blow, and the waters continually retreated from the face of the earth. Soon the ark came to rest on a mountain, Mount Ararat (Genesis 8:4). Sometimes, the winds blow in your life to dry up the waters so you may walk on dry land.

Noah sent a raven out after forty days, but the raven kept returning, so he knew the ground was not dry. Then he sent a dove, but the dove returned also, and he took her back into the ark. After seven more days, he sent the dove out again, and this time she returned with an olive leaf in her mouth. Noah knew the earth had dried. He waited another seven days and sent the dove out again. Noah knew it was time to leave the ark when the dove did not return.

Noah was 601 years old when he and his family disembarked from the ark at God's command to "be fruitful and multiply" (Genesis 8:15). Noah immediately built an altar to the Lord and offered a sacrifice of every clean beast and fowl (Genesis 8:20). That is a reminder to all men always to thank God for his deliverance. It was a sacrifice pleasing to the Lord. He made a covenant with Noah never to destroy every living thing on the face of the earth by flood again. "While the earth remaineth, seedtime and harvest, and cold and heat, and summer and winter, and day and night shall not cease" (Genesis 8:22).

God blessed Noah and his sons and gave them dominion over other living creatures. They were permitted to eat the vegetation that grew and animals but forbidden to eat the blood of animals. The blood of animals would be a substitutionary expiation for sin, but the blood of animals could only look towards the final sacrifice for sin, the blood of Jesus Christ.

God sealed the Noahic Covenant by setting a rainbow in the sky. It is a memorial of the covenant between Noah and God. When God looks upon it, he remembers his covenant, and mankind should remember it when he looks upon it.

And I will remember my covenant, which is between me and you and every living creature of all flesh; and the waters shall no more become a flood to destroy all flesh. And the bow shall be in the cloud; and I will look upon it, that I may remember the everlasting covenant between God and every living creature of all flesh that is upon the earth. And God said unto Noah, This is the token of the covenant, which I have established between me and all flesh that is upon the earth. (Genesis 9:15-17)

Noah lived 350 years after the flood. His total lifespan was 950 years. He was highly used of God. Through him, the human race was saved from extinction, and the promise that the woman's "seed" would crush the serpent's head continued (Genesis 3:15).

Noah's name means "rest." His parents, in giving him this name, said, "And he called his name Noah, saying, This same shall comfort us concerning our work and toil of our hands, because of the ground which the LORD hath cursed" (Genesis 5:29). In Christ we have a greater rest than the "rest" his parents had in Noah. Christ has secured a rest for the souls of those who believe. "Come unto me, all ye that labour and are heavy laden, and I will give you rest. Take my yoke upon you, and learn of me; for I am meek and lowly in heart: and ye shall find rest unto your souls. For my yoke is easy, and my burden is light" (Matthew 11:28-30).

Thank God for one righteous man, Noah, a force to be reckoned with, a formidable man.

3 ENOCH

By faith Enoch was translated that he should not see death; and was not found, because God had translated him: for before his translation he had this testimony, that he pleased God. (Hebrews 11:5)

Enoch had the greatest testimony that a man can have. He "walked with God and was not" (Genesis 5:24). He was translated and did not see death. Enoch's ascension foreshadows the ascension of Christ and those who will be resurrected and ascend in the rapture. He is one of only two men that did not see death. The other is Elijah, who ascended by a whirlwind.

Some scholars speculate that Enoch and Elijah are the two faithful witnesses in Revelation during the end times.

And I will give power unto my two witnesses, and they shall prophesy a thousand two hundred and threescore days, clothed in sackcloth. These are the two olive trees, and the two candlesticks standing before the God of the earth. (Revelation 11:3-4)

There are many other speculations as to who these two powerful witnesses might be, but this is not the place for that discussion. Enoch is listed as the seventh patriarch in the line of descent from Adam and is shown in the genealogy of Mary, the mother of our Lord.

Which was the son of Mathusala, which was the son of Enoch, which was the son of Jared, which was the son of Maleleel, which was the son of Cainan, Which was the son of Enos, which was the son of Seth, which was the son of Adam, which was the son of God. (Luke 3:37-38)

Enoch's lifespan was 365 years, the shortest of those listed in the genealogies before the flood, but his son, Methuselah, had the longest lifespan of anyone in the Bible, 969 years.

A man who walks with God is a man who walks with integrity. His faith in God is ever before him. No matter what others might say, he has the testimony that he pleases God. Walk on, O mighty man of God, until you walk into the Kingdom. You will become like Enoch, a force to be reckoned with, a formidable man.

4 ABRAHAM

Now the LORD had said unto Abram, Get thee out of thy country, and from thy kindred, and from thy father's house, unto a land that I will shew thee: And I will make of thee a great nation, and I will bless thee, and make thy name great; and thou shalt be a blessing: And I will bless them that bless thee, and curse him that curseth thee: and in thee shall all families of the earth be blessed.
(Genesis 12:1-3)

Consider just for a moment, if you will, the great patriarch Abraham. He was "the friend of God" (James 2:23); the father of the faithful (Romans 4:11, Galatians 3:6-9); the progenitor of the Israelites, Ishmaelites, Midianites, Edomites, and other people; and the recipient of the most important covenant made between God and humanity, known as the Abrahamic Covenant. Unique in scripture, he is an extraordinary demonstration of the principles of absolute faith in God and obedience to his commands. One would do well to read of him and do as he did when the Lord gave him the command to leave his home.

Abraham was born in Ur of the Chaldees (approximately 2000 – 1900 B.C.). Ur was a wealthy, well-populated city on the lower Euphrates River. His name was changed from Abram to Abraham ("father of multitudes"). His father, Terah, was a descendant of Shem. Terah migrated from the Ur of the Chaldees intending to go to the land of Canaan, but he settled in Haran and died before he could finish the journey. Haran lies to the north of the Euphrates-Tigris Rivers.

Abraham was divinely called by God to leave his kindred in Haran and travel "unto a land that I will shew thee." He was promised great blessings due to his obedience to the call. His call and obedience are of the utmost importance because God chose him to become the patriarch of ancient Israel, and from his lineage would spring the Messiah who would redeem mankind by shedding his blood on the cross for our sins.

The promises to Abraham were: 1) He would become a great nation; 2) God would make his name great; 3) he would be blessed; 4) he would be a blessing; 5) God would bless those that blessed him and curse those that cursed him; 6) all the families of the earth would be blessed in him; 7) and the land he tread on would be given to his descendants.

These promises were made to Abraham on an individual basis, as well as on a national basis, for his seed. The promise that all the earth would be blessed in him prophesies that Christ would come into the world through his descendants and are, therefore, a universal promise. All mankind has truly been blessed through his obedience.

The Abrahamic Covenant would be further defined, renewed, ratified, and confirmed several times during Abraham's life, but the basic tenets remained the same: blessings for him and his descendants, land his descendants would inherit, numerous descendants, and most importantly, God's redemptive dealings with humanity would flow through his lineage. In addition to these basics, circumcision was later instituted as a seal of the covenant (Genesis 17:10-14). This covenant is eternal and permanent in nature. All other covenants regarding salvation flow from it: the Messiah is promised in the Old Covenant and presented in the New Covenant. It is based upon God's grace toward Israel and Abraham's faith and acceptance. It is still in force and effect to those who believe the Savior has come. We are engrafted into the family of Abraham by faith in Christ and become inheritors of the promises. "And if ye be Christ's, then are ye Abraham's seed, and heirs according to the promise" (Galatians 3:29).

Abraham "believed in the LORD; and he counted it to him for righteousness" (Genesis 15:6; Romans 4:3, 22.) He was 75 years old when he left Haran with his wife, his nephew Lot, and all they owned to go into the land of Canaan. At this time, he had no children on which to base the promises of God on; but he walked by faith. "By faith Abraham, when he was called to go out into a place which he should after receive for an inheritance, obeyed; and he went out, not knowing whither he went" (Hebrews 11:8). He kept the faith and became the father of Isaac, the heir of the promise; Isaac became the father of Jacob, who was renamed Israel. From the loins of Israel sprang the twelve tribes of Israel, each of whom became a nation.

God chose Abraham to become the father of the Messianic nation, and his faith justified him. Righteousness was imputed to him. "But for us also, to whom it shall be imputed, if we believe on him that raised up Jesus our Lord from the dead; Who was delivered for our offences, and was raised again for our justification" Romans 4:23, 24). When we accept the finished work of Christ in our lives, we become the children of Abraham, an act achieved only through the blood of Christ. Moreover, we are reconciled to the Father and have access to the throne of God, Christ being our mediator. Abraham was a type of Christ. In him, all the nations of the earth were blessed. He was used mightily by God to foretell the promise of the coming of Christ and his lineage to carry the seed of the promise. Christ is the great antitype.

Abraham was representative of many nations, especially Israel; all the promises made to Him were made in respect of that position. Christ represents all people from every nation, tribe, and language. His death on the cross fulfilled the promises to Abraham of the Covenant of Grace. This receiver of the Covenant was a force to be reckoned with, a formidable man.

5 ISAAC

And God said, Sarah thy wife shall bear thee a son indeed; and thou shalt call his name Isaac: and I will establish my covenant with him for an everlasting covenant, and with his seed after him. (Genesis 17:19)

Isaac means "laughter." It was foretold to Abraham that Sarah would bear him a son, and his name would be Isaac. Both Sarah and Abraham laughed because it seemed impossible that they would know such joy. Sarah was beyond the childbearing age.

Abraham and Sarah waited a long time for a child to be born. Sarah tried to offer an alternative through Abraham having a child by her maid, Hagar, but wasn't very happy with the behavior of her maid when she became pregnant. Perhaps Hagar knew what the covenant meant and thought to take the place of Sarah as the mother of Abraham's children. At long last and finally, a child was born to Abraham and Sarah: the son of Promise, the seed of Abraham, the apple of Sarah's eye, and heir to the Abrahamic Covenant and all its benefits.

Isaac was born "at the set time of which God had spoken to" Abraham (Genesis 21:2). He was born at the time God planned him to be born. He was not born before that time. He was not born after that time. He was born according to the time God set for him to be born. Abraham gave him the name God told him to give him, Isaac (Genesis 21:3). Now Abraham and Sarah's joy was full.

There may be promises in your life that have not manifested yet. Know that at the set time, you will see them fulfilled. Hold on to God's unchanging hand!

Per the Covenant of Circumcision, Abraham circumcised Isaac when he was eight days old. Abraham was 100 years old, and Sarah was 90 when their son was born. "And Sarah said, God hath made me to laugh, so that all that hear will laugh with me. And she said, Who would have said unto Abraham, that Sarah should have given children suck? for I have born him a son in his old age" (Genesis 21:6-7). Isaac was a true miracle!

Ishmael, the son of Hagar, was sent away by demand of Sarah. Abraham had hesitated to do so. God assured Abraham that Ishmael would also be great, but his covenant would be with Isaac.

Isaac showed a strong faith, even when that of his father was tested. God told Abraham to take his only son to the land of Moriah and offer him as a burnt offering upon the mountain (Genesis 22:2).

By faith Abraham, when he was tried, offered up Isaac: and he that had received the promises offered up **his**

only begotten son, Of whom it was said, That in Isaac shall thy seed be called: Accounting that God was able to raise him up, even from the dead; from whence also he received him in a figure. (Hebrews 11:17-19)

Isaac carried the wood, the knife, and the fire for his own sacrifice. It has been compared to Christ carrying his own cross on the way to the crucifixion.

Isaac wondered where the lamb was for the sacrifice, but he had full faith in his father that "God will provide himself a lamb for a burnt offering" (Genesis 22:8). His trust in his father was equal to Abraham's trust in his heavenly Father. We should all have such trust in our Father.

As his father prepared to slay him with the knife, an angel of the Lord stayed his hand. Abraham lifted his eyes and saw a ram caught in a bush and offered the ram in the place of his son.

Our Father in heaven has offered his only begotten son in our place. His blood was the only blood worthy of taking away the sins of the world. Little Isaac's blood could never have sufficed.

The Road of Redemption was paved with the Hebrew patriarchs but would not continue without descendants. After Sarah died, Abraham arranged a marriage for Isaac with the daughter of her brother. His servant traveled to his home, choosing Rebekah as Isaac's wife by divine guidance. He asked for a sign and the sign was given just as he had asked. God is a God of exactness. What he said, he will surely perform.

Isaac loved the beautiful Rebekah the moment he saw her, but she turned out to be barren as his mother had been. He was forty years old when he married Rebekah, but they had been married twenty years, and no heir was born. With great faith, Isaac did as all men would be wise to do. He prayed for his wife. All men should stand in the gap for their families and loved ones. Pray until you move Heaven.

Rebekah conceived, and after a troublesome pregnancy, twins were born, Esau and Jacob. They struggled within their mother's womb and would struggle greatly in life. It was for control of the Abrahamic Covenant. Both would be great, but the covenant had been promised to Jacob before he was born. Isaac, when he was old, sought to bless the elder son but was circumvented by the conniving trickery of his dear wife, Rebekah. Yet through it all, God was in control. Rebekah could not succeeded in her plans if God had not willed Jacob to become the heir and the third person in the triumvirate of patriarchs of Israel: Abraham, Isaac, and Jacob.

Isaac, the second person in that great Hebrew triumvirate, was a force to be reckoned with, a formidable man.

6 JACOB

And Joseph brought in Jacob his father, and set him before Pharaoh: and Jacob blessed Pharaoh. And Pharaoh said unto Jacob, How old art thou? And Jacob said unto Pharaoh, The days of the years of my pilgrimage are an hundred and thirty years: few and evil have the days of the years of my life been, and have not attained unto the days of the years of the life of my fathers in the days of their pilgrimage. And Jacob blessed Pharaoh, and went out from before Pharaoh.
(Genesis 47:7-10)

Jacob is the third of the patriarchs in the line of descent of the Hebrew people. His beginning did not seem to foreshadow greatness. He was born to his parents when they were older. His mother had been barren. He was the second birth of twins, but he was the apple of his mother's eye, while his brother Esau was the favorite of his father, Isaac.

The twins struggled in their mother's womb and continued their struggle in life until it reached a boiling point when Jacob stole the patriarchal blessing from his brother, aided and abetted by his mastermind of a mother. Jacob was sent off to relatives to find a wife and give his brother a cooling-off period. It would be twenty years before he returned.

At this point, one would have thought Jacob's plight might seem hopeless, having stolen his brother's birthright and blessing. His name means "supplanter," and it was apt to what his character was. But Jacob had the blessing, and once it was conferred, it could not be revoked. The blessing of the Abrahamic Covenant was passed to Jacob, and by that act, he became the third person in the Hebrew triumvirate: "The God of Abraham, the God of Isaac, the God of Jacob." It will thunder down through the halls of history until the end of time.

One may well have wondered just how Jacob would finish his course after all this turmoil. On his way to Padanaram, he had a dream. It was an awesome dream. Jacob saw a ladder reaching from the earth to heaven with angels ascending and descending on it. Some say the ladder symbolized the one mediator between God and man, the Lord Jesus Christ. God told Jacob, "I am the Lord God of Abraham thy father, and the God of Isaac ...." God himself affirmed the Abrahamic Covenant with him. In addition, the Lord promised to be with him and to keep him wherever he went.

In Padanaram, Jacob was smitten with love when he first laid eyes on the beautiful Rachel. He served seven years for Rachel's hand in marriage, but he awakened the morning after his wedding to find that it was not Rachel he was married to but her sister, Leah. His father-in-law, Laban, had treated him shamefully. A week later, Jacob was allowed to marry Rachel after promising to work for seven more years.

We saw Jacob begin to mature from Rebekah's son into a father, but there was dysfunction in his family. Jacob loved Rachel more than he loved Leah, which showed in his treatment of the two women. Leah eventually birthed six of the patriarchs of the twelve tribes of Israel, but Jacob never, ever loved her the way he loved Rachel. Jacob had grown, but he had not yet arrived at his destiny.

Jacob became wealthy. He prospered no matter how Laban tried to cheat him. After 20 years, Jacob left Laban and returned home to reconcile with Esau. On his way home, he wrestled with an angel. He prevailed, and his name was changed to Israel "for as a prince hast thou power with God and with men and hast prevailed." (Genesis 32:28).

It was a reconciliation that stands out as one of the greatest reconciliations ever recorded. It gives us, who may need to reconcile with a loved one, much hope. The same Esau who had promised to kill his brother without ceremony ran to meet Jacob. He warmly embraced Jacob and he kissed him. As these two brothers stood embracing one another, they both wept. It was a foreshadow of the reconciliation between Joseph and his brothers, the sons of Jacob. The boys were now men. As we looked at these two men embracing, we knew that was what genuine forgiveness looked like. This is a foreshadowing of the reconciliation of sinners to the Father. His arms are wide open. You have only to repent and accept his substitutionary death on the cross.

Jacob's troubles were not over. He settled in Shechem, where two of his sons destroyed the city, killing all the men because the prince of the city had ravished their sister. They left Shechem under divine protection. The allies of Shechem feared them. This family carried the royal seed, and the blessing of God was upon them, creating an invisible shield. Sadly, Rachel died in childbirth with her second son, Benjamin, on the trip to Bethel.

Jacob had twelve sons by Leah, Rachel, and their two maids. His favorite was Joseph, the eldest son of Rachel. Like his parents before him, he showed blatant favoritism, even making Joseph a special coat of colors like that kings would wear. His favoritism towards Joseph caused dissension, and the brothers sold Joseph into slavery. Jacob was grieved. He endured twenty-two years lost in grief, believing his son, Joseph, to be dead.

For Jacob, it was heartbreak, but for Joseph, every step took him toward his destiny as the second ruler over all of Egypt and as a Savior for his people and the known world during a worldwide famine.

Jacob and his family were suffering amid a famine. Jacob heard there was food in Egypt and sent his sons to buy provisions. Joseph recognized his brothers, and; after a few tests to see if they had changed and were trustworthy, he revealed himself to them in a dramatic reconciliation. Joseph sent for Jacob and his entire family to move to Egypt. What a reunion between father and son.

What a healing moment when tears washed away years of despair. Jacob brought his own goods and livestock into Egypt, which were substantial, but they were nothing compared to this great nation.

Our opening verse in this chapter sees Jacob at the epitome of his journey. He is presented to Pharaoh as royalty, being the father of Joseph. The journey had sometimes been difficult. He had endured trials and tribulations. But that was his journey. What he endured were the experiences that had given him the wisdom to know his purpose in life. This was the path from which he ascended to greatness. We all have a journey. We all have a purpose to fulfill. If your journey has sometimes been difficult, if you have endured trials and tribulations, just hold on. God has a purpose for your pain.

Here we see a mature Jacob before Pharaoh, a wiser Jacob, one kept by the power of God. He is no longer Rebekah's baby; he is no longer a boy. He has stepped into his royal role as Israel, the progenitor of the Twelve Tribes of Israel. We see in this epic scene a ruler before a ruler, a king before a king, and majesty before majesty. How do we know? Because the Bible says the Lion of the Tribe of Judah sprang from his loins, the Mighty One of Jacob, the Root of David, the Chief Ruler, "the blessed and only Potentate, the King of kings, and Lord of lords!" (2 Timothy 6:15.)

So "Jacob blessed Pharaoh." He blessed Pharaoh coming in, and he blessed him going out. I would remind you, just briefly, of Abraham when he met Melchizedek, king and priest of Salem, and gave him tithes of all he had from the spoils of war after he had slaughtered the kings that kidnapped his nephew, Lot. Melchizedek blessed Abraham (Genesis 14:19).

Hebrews 7:7 sums it up this way: "And without all contradiction the less is blessed of the better."

"And without all contradiction," meaning an admitted principle, a point that cannot be challenged, a principle that stands on its own for all time and will never be repealed, it is beyond dispute.

"…the less is blessed of the better." The one of superior rank blesses the one of lesser rank. As Melchizedek was superior in rank to Abraham, so Jacob had a higher authority than Pharaoh.

Though one wondered at times, Jacob is finishing well. Here is Jacob, the priest, prophet, patriarch, and prince of God, before Pharaoh. Here is Jacob, who carries the Abrahamic Covenant blessing. Here is Jacob come into the fullness of his glory. And he blesses Pharaoh. Make no mistake. This is the priestly blessing given by divine authority. "And without all contradiction, the less is blessed of the better."

"For when we were yet without strength, in due time Christ died for the ungodly." (Romans 5:6). Christ died for the irreconcilable, for the dysfunctional family. He died for the thief and backstabber. He died for Abraham, Isaac, and Jacob, and he died for you and for me. We have truly been blessed. We have been made joint-heirs with Christ. We have been made a royal priesthood, kings, and queens.

I submit to you with absolute certainty, with indisputable truth, with irrefutable conviction, with incontrovertible evidence, beyond a shadow of a doubt, without any fear of retribution, "And without all contradiction, the less is blessed of the better."

7 JOSEPH

And Joseph's master took him, and put him into the prison, a place where the king's prisoners were bound: and he was there in the prison. But the LORD was with Joseph, and shewed him mercy, and gave him favour in the sight of the keeper of the prison (Genesis 39:20-21).

Joseph, the dreamer and visionary, was hated by his brothers because his father loved him best, and his dreams showed they would be subservient to him. Let's face it. Hate is a mild word for how Joseph's brother felt for their father's outright favoritism toward Joseph and his "more righteous than thou" attitude they deemed he had. They despised the ground he walked on.

When their father sent Joseph to check on them while they were shepherding, it created the perfect storm. They saw him coming, knew he would go back and rat them out, and their hatred was stirred into a flame. They took advantage of the situation and quickly planned his demise. They imprisoned him in a pit and sat down to eat. Some traders were coming through and Judah said they should sell Joseph instead of killing him and having his blood on their hands. Joseph was sold to the traders who took him to Egypt and sold him to Potiphar, one of Pharaoh's chief officers and captain of his guard. We know his story well. Potiphar saw that the Lord was with Joseph and made him steward over all that he owned. Through trickery, Potiphar's wife had him cast into prison.

It would seem that Joseph's dreams had not only been deferred but altogether derailed. Yet even in prison, he rose to the highest level and was set over the affairs of the jail. There he met and interpreted the dreams of two of Pharoah's former household employees. Just as Joseph said, one was restored to his former duties, and the other was executed.

It took a while, but the employee who had been restored to his duties remembered Joseph and recommended him to Pharoah when Pharoah had a dream he did not know the meaning of, and his wise men could not tell him. Joseph was recognized by Pharoah and moved up from a prisoner to the second most powerful position in the country. God used him to save people from a severe famine, including his brothers, who had sold him into slavery.

Joseph recognized his brothers when they came to Egypt to buy supplies and reconciled with them after a series of tests. He sent for his father, and they embraced after years of grief. Joseph provided shelter for his family in the best land in Egypt. They lived as royalty. Jacob was given a funeral as one of the royalties of the land, and his body was carried back to Shechem and buried in the cave Abraham bought to bury Sarah in.

And Joseph said unto them, Fear not: for am I in the place of God? But as for you, ye thought evil against me; but God meant it unto good, to bring to pass, as it is this day, to save much people alive. Now therefore fear ye not: I will nourish you, and your little ones. And he comforted them, and spake kindly unto them. And Joseph dwelt in Egypt, he, and his father's house: and Joseph lived an hundred and ten years. (Genesis 50:19-22)

Joseph's brothers wondered if Joseph might take vengeance upon them when Jacob was gone, but Joseph assured them he would not. Joseph foresaw that Israel would one day leave Egypt and commanded that his body be carried out with them when they left for the Promised Land.

Joseph's sufferings, trials, and persecutions were only the steps and means God used to take him to the realization of the vision. It was not deferred, it was not derailed, and it was not even delayed. It was right on course. Know that God has not forgotten you. Your vision has not been deferred, it has not been derailed, and it has not even been delayed. It is right on course. "For the vision is yet for an appointed time, but at the end it shall speak, and not lie: though it tarry, wait for it; because it will surely come, it will not tarry" (Habakkuk 2:3). Joseph was a force to be reckoned with, a formidable man.

8 JUDAH

Judah, thou art he whom thy brethren shall praise: thy hand shall be in the neck of thine enemies; thy father's children shall bow down before thee. Judah is a lion's whelp: from the prey, my son, thou art gone up: he stooped down, he couched as a lion, and as an old lion; who shall rouse him up? The sceptre shall not depart from Judah, nor a lawgiver from between his feet, until Shiloh come; and unto him shall the gathering of the people be. Binding his foal unto the vine, and his ass's colt unto the choice vine; he washed his garments in wine, and his clothes in the blood of grapes: His eyes shall be red with wine, and his teeth white with milk.
(Genesis 49:8-12)

Judah (Yehuda in Hebrew) was the fourth son born to Jacob and Leah. His name means "praise" "And she conceived again, and bare a son: and she said, Now will I praise the LORD: therefore she called his name Judah; and left bearing" (Genesis 29:35). He is the fourth patriarch in the line of descent of our Savior. His was the royal lineage, but it did not always seem that way.

Judah was with his brothers when they sold Joseph into slavery. He convinced his brothers that killing Joseph would not profit them.

And Judah said unto his brethren, What profit is it if we slay our brother, and conceal his blood? Come, and let us sell him to the Ishmeelites, and let not our hand be upon him; for he is our brother and our flesh. And his brethren were content. (Genesis 37:26-27)

Judah's firstborn, Er, was so evil that God killed him, and he promised his wife, Tamar, to give her his son Onan to have children and raise them up. This law was enacted among the Hebrew people even before it was written into the Mosaic Law.

If brethren dwell together, and one of them die, and have no child, the wife of the dead shall not marry without unto a stranger: her husband's brother shall go in unto her, and take her to him to wife, and perform the duty of an husband's brother unto her. And it shall be, that the firstborn which she beareth shall succeed in the name of his brother which is dead, that his name be not put out of Israel. (Deuteronomy 25:5-6)

Onan sinned by spilling his seed on the ground, and God was not pleased. He died also. Judah then promised Tamar his youngest son, Shelah, when he came of age. He asked her to return to her parent's house until then. He may have been putting her off because he was afraid that something would happen to Shelah.

Judah's wife died, and Tamar heard he was going to

shear his sheep. She tricked him into impregnating her by pretending to be a prostitute on the side of the road. When Judah heard she was pregnant, he sent for her intending to have her killed for the sin of adultery against his son. He had not released her from her vows. Tamar had been wise enough to secure Judah's staff, bracelets, and signet ring as security for her price and sent them to him, telling the men he sent that the man they belonged to was her child's father.

Judah was shocked. He accepted that he was the father and remembered his promise to Tamar to give her his son Shelah in marriage. He never touched her again. Tamar birthed twins for Judah. Both are shown in the genealogy of Jesus in Matthew. The youngest, Phares, is in the direct lineage of the Christ.

Joseph had been taken from the pit and sold to traders. The traders sold him to Potiphar, the captain of Pharaoh's guard. Potiphar's wife had him thrown into prison through trickery. In prison, he was given charge over the other prisoners. He was released to appear before Pharaoh after one of the King's employees told him Joseph had interpreted a dream for him while in prison. Joseph interpreted the dream of the King. There would be seven years of plenty and seven years of famine. He was decorated, honored, made the second highest power in the country, and put in control of preparing for the famine.

The famine was throughout the land. Jacob sent Judah and his brothers to buy food in Egypt after hearing there was food there. Joseph recognized his brothers and tested them to see if they had changed. Joseph refused to provide further food for the family if they did not bring their youngest brother with them when they returned to Egypt. We see Judah emerging as the leader of the family. One could see he had matured.

> And Judah said unto Israel his father, Send the lad with me, and we will arise and go; that we may live, and not die, both we, and thou, and also our little ones. I will be surety for him; of my hand shalt thou require him: if I bring him not unto thee, and set him before thee, then let me bear the blame for ever. (Genesis 43:8-9)

Judah reminded his father that they could not return to Egypt without Benjamin. He assured him he would personally guarantee Benjamin's safety and that Jacob could fully blame him if anything happened. He put his own life on the line for his brother. Over the years, God had been at work in Judah's life, performing a work in him that he would also finish. God is at work in your life. He is performing a work in you that he will also finish. You shall come forth as pure gold.

Joseph tested his brothers by setting a trap that indicated Benjamin had taken Joseph's cup. Joseph's servants took Benjamin into custody, and all the brothers returned with him. The lawgiver in Judah stood up, and he eloquently defended his brother.

> And we said unto my lord, We have a father, an old man, and a child of his old age, a little one; and his brother is dead, and he alone is left of his mother, and his father loveth him. And thou saidst unto thy servants, Bring him down unto me, that I may set mine eyes upon

him. And we said unto my lord, The lad cannot leave his father: for if he should leave his father, his father would die. And thou saidst unto thy servants, Except your youngest brother come down with you, ye shall see my face no more. (Genesis 44:20-23)

He explained that they could not come home without Benjamin, or their father would surely die from sorrow. His summation was powerful.

Now therefore, I pray thee, let thy servant abide instead of the lad a bondman to my lord; and let the lad go up with his brethren. For how shall I go up to my father, and the lad be not with me? lest peradventure I see the evil that shall come on my father. (Genesis 44:33-34)

Judah offered to take his brother's place and be a bondservant. He could not face his father without Benjamin because he had given himself as surety. He would cause his father's death if he returned without him.

His plea touched the heart of Joseph, and he could no longer refrain from his emotions in front of his brothers. He ordered everyone out of the room except his brothers. He revealed himself in one of the most dramatic scenes in the Bible. The reconciliation would have surely touched their mothers' hearts had they still been alive. Judah and his brothers returned home and then went back to live in Egypt with their father and their families.

At the end of his days, Jacob gathered his sons and prophesied what would happen when they came out of Egypt. He prophesied the blessings and the inheritance of

Judah (Genesis 49:8-12). His was the royalty, the scepter, the leadership. His brothers would praise him. The Davidic dynasty would spring from Judah. The grace of God was upon him, and it became evident when he offered himself as a substitute for Benjamin. In so doing, Judah is seen as a type of Christ. His greatest descendant would one day become a substitute for the sins of the world. Christ, the Messiah, is the greater Judah, the antitype. "I Jesus have sent mine angel to testify unto you these things in the churches. I am the root and the offspring of David, and the bright and morning star" (Revelation 22:16). Judah was a force to be reckoned with, a formidable man.

9 MOSES

And there arose not a prophet since in Israel like unto Moses, whom the LORD knew face to face, In all the signs and the wonders, which the LORD sent him to do in the land of Egypt to Pharaoh, and to all his servants, and to all his land, And in all that mighty hand, and in all the great terror which Moses shewed in the sight of all Israel. (Deuteronomy 34:10-12)

Moses is one of the most important men ever to have been born. A descendant of Levi, he was Israel's great lawgiver and deliverer, the mediator of the Old Covenant, and is considered the greatest prophet in Judaism, Islam, Christianity, and other religions. He is also considered the greatest writer ever to have lived, having been used of God to write the Torah, the first five books of the Bible.

Moses was born during a time when Pharaoh had issued an edict that all male Hebrew babies be killed at birth. The midwives he first ordered to do it feared God more than they feared disobeying his order, so he ordered any

Egyptian who knew of one to kill him. Jochebed, the mother of Moses, hid him until it became too dangerous. She then made him a basket and placed him near the banks of the river where the daughter of Pharaoh came every day with his sister, Miriam, to watch what would happen.

Pharaoh's daughter saw something special about the child and took him as her own. She sent Miriam to get a wet nurse for him, and she got her mother, who nursed her son. When he was weaned, she took him to Pharaoh's daughter. He was raised as a prince and given the education of a prince.

"(Now the man Moses was very meek, above all the men which were upon the face of the earth.)" (Numbers 12:3.) Meekness is sometimes construed as weakness. It is merely power under control. Moses was meek, but he was not weak. He was a defender of the weak. Seeing one of his Hebrew brothers being beaten by a taskmaster one day, he killed the man. The deed went unappreciated. People you try to help will not always accept it in the manner you gave it. Help them anyway. The next day when Moses tried to resolve a conflict between two Hebrews arguing, they turned against him.

> And he said, Who made thee a prince and a judge over us? Intendest thou to kill me, as thou killedst the Egyptian? And Moses feared, and said, Surely this thing is known. (Exodus 2:14)

Pharaoh heard about it and wanted Moses executed. Moses fled to the land of Midian, where he defended the priest's daughters from men who would take the water they had drawn for their animals and give it to theirs to drink. He was given Zipporah, one of seven daughters of the priest, in marriage.

Moses was tending his father-in-law's flock on Mount Horeb when he saw a bush on fire but not consumed. He went up to it for a closer inspection, and God spoke to him from the midst of the bush. Moses was given a divine commission to be the vessel used of God to deliver the children of Israel from bondage. He was hesitant to accept this great calling. God gave him his older brother, Aaron as a spokesperson to speak through, and Moses finally stepped into the position as the greatest civil rights leader the world has ever known.

By the mighty hand of God, under the leadership of Moses, the children of Israel were freed. They received reparations for their years of slavery. They crossed the Red Sea on foot while the host of Pharaoh drowned. But they still had the mindset of slavery, and the journey was not easy. At every test, they grumbled, and God provided a miracle. He provided Bread from Heaven to feed them, water from a stone to quench their thirst, and many other miraculous blessings.

Only two returned a positive report when Moses sent twelve men to spy on the Promised Land. The others feared the giant stature of the occupants in the land. They rebelled against Moses, and God heard them. Moses interceded on their behalf, and God spared them, but only two of those who were twenty years and over would be allowed to enter the Promised Land, the two who bought back good reports, Caleb and Joshua.

Your carcases shall fall in this wilderness; and all that were numbered of you, according to your whole number, from twenty years old and upward, which have murmured against me, Doubtless ye shall not come into the land, concerning which I sware to make you dwell therein, save Caleb the son of Jephunneh, and Joshua the son of Nun. But your little ones, which ye said should be a prey, them will I bring in, and they shall know the land which ye have despised. (Numbers 14:29-31)

Israel would wander in the wilderness for forty years. Those twenty years old and above who murmured against the Lord would die during those years.

In the last stage of their journey, they came to Kadesh, where Miriam died. There was no water there, and the people complained against Moses and Aaron. They remembered Egypt and longed to return. Their fond memories of Egypt are not accurate. They were oppressed. Their children were murdered there. They cried out to the Lord, and he delivered them. He had helped them through miraculous acts during their wilderness travels. Now, as they are beginning the last stage of their journey, they are complaining as they did at the beginning and throughout.

When, on your journey, you experience hardship, struggles, heartache, and pain, when friends and loved ones abandon you, do as Moses and Aaron did. They took it to the Lord.

And Moses and Aaron went from the presence of the assembly unto the door of the tabernacle of the congregation, and they fell upon their faces: and the glory of the LORD appeared unto them. (Numbers 20:6)

As men of God, as leaders, as fathers, as the children of God, you must turn to him for guidance in every situation. The songwriter wrote a song about letting Jesus lead you. "Let Jesus lead you all the way."

Aaron and Moses prostrated themselves before the Lord, and the Shekinah Glory appeared. O mighty man, you can't fight this war on your strength. The fight is not against flesh and blood. It is against principalities and authorities in high places. The battle is not yours. It's the Lords. Let him fight for you.

Be very careful to obey the instructions exactly as the Lord gives them to you. 99.9999 percent of obedience is disobedience. You will be held accountable for the least disobedience.

And the LORD spake unto Moses, saying, Take the rod, and gather thou the assembly together, thou, and Aaron thy brother, and speak ye unto the rock before their eyes; and it shall give forth his water, and thou shalt bring forth to them water out of the rock: so thou shalt give the congregation, and their beasts drink. (Numbers 20:7-8)

The instructions were very clear. All Moses was told to do was to take the rod of God and gather the people and Aaron. Then he was to "speak" to the rock before them, and water would gush forth. Simple as that.

Every leader, every child of God, and every individual has a point where they become frustrated. Because Moses was a humble man and a great leader, it does not mean he was perfect. It had been a hard, long, arduous forty years in the wilderness with a stubborn, ungrateful people. Moses did almost as he was told to do. He took the rod, and he gathered the people. But then he lost control. He just had to get something off of his chest.

> And Moses and Aaron gathered the congregation together before the rock, and he said unto them, Hear now, ye rebels; must we fetch you water out of this rock? And Moses lifted up his hand, and with his rod he smote the rock twice: and the water came out abundantly, and the congregation drank, and their beasts also. (Numbers 20:10-11)

Moses was supposed to speak to the rock, but he became irate and struck it not once but twice. He lost his patience at the disbelief of the people. Sure, the waters flowed, and the congregation and their animals drank, but there was a penalty for the disobedience of Moses, and Aaron would also be held accountable.

> And the LORD spake unto Moses and Aaron, Because ye believed me not, to sanctify me in the eyes of the children of Israel, therefore ye shall not bring this congregation into the land which I have given them. (Numbers 20:12)

The strikes against the rock were not what God had commanded in this case. They were unwarranted. Jesus took upon himself unwarranted stripes for our sake.

But he was wounded for our transgressions, he was bruised for our iniquities: the chastisement of our peace was upon him; and with his stripes we are healed. (Isaiah 53:5)

Moses had walked in his integrity every step of the way for forty years. Moses showed he was only human. He had a temporary breakdown, a moment of disobedience, such a small step outside of the instructions of God. For this lapse of judgment, for this act outside of his character, for this disobedience, he and Aaron forfeited the privilege of bringing the children of Israel into the Promised Land. So close, and yet, so far away.

But when you recall Moses and Aaron, remember their great works for the Lord and their lives of integrity and know that you, too, are capable of misstepping. The best of us are only human beings. There but for the grace of God, there but for his mercy, there but for his kindness, there but for his everlasting compassion, there but for the blood of Christ, go you and me.

Moses, the deliverer of his people, prophesied of a prophet to come who would be like him. Moses spoke to God face to face as a friend to a friend, but he was not the one to come. "The LORD thy God will raise up unto thee a Prophet from the midst of thee, of thy brethren, like unto me; unto him ye shall hearken" (Deuteronomy 18:15). God used Moses in a powerful way to deliver his people from slavery. Christ is the greater deliverer and the one Mediator between God and man. He fulfilled the law of Moses, brought grace and mercy for a sinful people, and delivered us from this world's evils.

Wherefore, holy brethren, partakers of the heavenly calling, consider the Apostle and High Priest of our profession, Christ Jesus; who was faithful to him that appointed him, as also Moses was faithful in all his house. For this man was counted worthy of more glory than Moses, inasmuch as he who hath builded the house hath more honour than the house. (Hebrews 3:1-3).

Moses was not allowed to go into the Promised Land with the Children of Israel, but he was allowed to view it. After giving his farewell and final prophecies, he climbed Mount Nebo, and the Lord showed him the Promised Land.

And the LORD said unto him, This is the land which I sware unto Abraham, unto Isaac, and unto Jacob, saying, I will give it unto thy seed: I have caused thee to see it with thine eyes, but thou shalt not go over thither. So Moses the servant of the LORD died there in the land of Moab, according to the word of the LORD. And he buried him in a valley in the land of Moab, over against Bethpeor: but no man knoweth of his sepulchre unto this day. And Moses was an hundred and twenty years old when he died: his eye was not dim, nor his natural force abated. (Deuteronomy 34:4-7)

Moses died and was buried by the Lord. Some scholars believe that the grave was not made known because the people might have made it a place of worship and Moses, an idol god, for he was a king among his people.

Moses commanded us a law, even the inheritance of the congregation of Jacob. And he was king in Jeshurun, when the heads of the people and the tribes of Israel were gathered together. (Deuteronomy 33:4-5)

Moses did what all men in leadership should do. He anointed the next leader before his death and mentored him.

And Joshua the son of Nun was full of the spirit of wisdom; for Moses had laid his hands upon him: and the children of Israel hearkened unto him, and did as the LORD commanded Moses. (Deuteronomy 34:9)

At 120, Moses still had all the vigor and strength of his youth when he died. So Moses, the great lawgiver, the great prophet, the great writer of the Torah, the great friend of the Great God, the great deliverer of his people died, and all Israel stopped to weep and mourn for thirty days. He was a force to be reckoned with, a formidable man.

10 AARON

And the children of Israel, even the whole congregation, journeyed from Kadesh, and came unto mount Hor. And the LORD spake unto Moses and Aaron in mount Hor, by the coast of the land of Edom, saying, Aaron shall be gathered unto his people: for he shall not enter into the land which I have given unto the children of Israel, because ye rebelled against my word at the water of Meribah. (Numbers 20:22-24)

Aaron had done all that was assigned into his hands and was to be "gathered unto his people." But let us pause to consider the life of Aaron, the first Great High Priest of Israel and a prophet of the Lord.

Aaron was the older brother of Moses. He was the second child born to his parents.

And the name of Amram's wife was Jochebed, the daughter of Levi, whom her mother bare to Levi in Egypt: and she bare unto Amram Aaron and Moses, and Miriam their sister. (Numbers 26:59)

We were first introduced to Aaron in Exodus.

> And the anger of the LORD was kindled against Moses, and he said, Is not Aaron the Levite thy brother? I know that he can speak well. And also, behold, he cometh forth to meet thee: and when he seeth thee, he will be glad in his heart. (Exodus 4:14)

For whatever reason, Moses was unwilling to readily accept his appointment to lead the Children of Israel out of Egypt. God's anger was kindled after patiently answering all of the objections and excuses Moses threw up to him. He gave Aaron as a spokesperson to the people. Moses would be the spokesman to Aaron.

> And the LORD said to Aaron, Go into the wilderness to meet Moses. And he went, and met him in the mount of God, and kissed him. And Moses told Aaron all the words of the LORD who had sent him, and all the signs which he had commanded him. And Moses and Aaron went and gathered together all the elders of the children of Israel: And Aaron spake all the words which the LORD had spoken unto Moses, and did the signs in the sight of the people. (Exodus 4:27-30)

For the most part, Aaron obeyed the laws and followed in his brother's footsteps. He had allowed the people to pressure him into building the golden calf when they thought Moses might not have been returning to the camp while he was with God on Mount Sinai (Exodus 32:1-3) receiving the tablets inscribed with the commandments. He was involved in a conspiracy against Moses' leadership led by their sister, Miriam, which God quickly ended

(Numbers 12:1-12). But these acts did not prevent him from entering the Promised Land. It was the rebellion of leadership at Meribah. As a man, you are a leader of your family, perhaps in your church, community, or job. You are accountable to God.

The prophet, Micah, attests that Aaron was given authority from God and recognized as a prophet in his own right.

> For I brought thee up out of the land of Egypt, and redeemed thee out of the house of servants; and I sent before thee Moses, Aaron, and Miriam. (Micah 6:4)

Aaron's historical significance comes from being appointed the first Great High Priest of Israel.

> And take thou unto thee Aaron thy brother, and his sons with him, from among the children of Israel, that he may minister unto me in the priest's office, even Aaron, Nadab and Abihu, Eleazar and Ithamar, Aaron's sons. (Exodus 28:1)

Understand that the priesthood was not bestowed upon women but men, and more specifically, only upon Aaron and his sons and their descendants. The male Levites were given to them as gifts. They were for the support of the priesthood for their responsibilities were many.

> And I, behold, I have taken your brethren the Levites from among the children of Israel: to you they are given as a gift for the LORD, to do the service of the tabernacle of the congregation. (Numbers 18:6)

"And Aaron took him Elisheba, daughter of Amminadab, sister of Naashon, to wife; and she bare him Nadab, and Abihu, Eleazar, and Ithamar" (6:23). Aaron married Elisheba. Elisheba is the same name as Elizabeth. It means "the oath of the Lord." She was the daughter of Amminadab and the sister of Naashon, captain of the children of Judah (Numbers 2:1-4).

The marriage of Aaron and Elisheba created an alliance between the royal family and the priestly family and was the beginning of the entire Levitical Priesthood. Amminadab, the father of Elisheba, was the prince of the tribe of Judah, an ancestor of Christ. He was Judah's great-great-great-grandson and Boaz's great-grandfather, a predecessor of David the King (Matthew 1:3-6).

Elisheba's brother, Naashon, became prince after his father and was chosen as chief commander of the host of the children Judah, who would lead the military procession guarding the Tabernacle and Levites as they traveled to the Promised Land.

Four sons were born to Aaron and Elisheba: Nadab, Abihu, Eleazar, and Ithamar. Nadab and Abihu, the two oldest, perished on the very day Aaron, and they were consecrated to the Lord for offering strange fire (Leviticus 10:1-2). They violated a sacred ordinance, and fire went out from the presence of God and consumed them. Eleazar succeeded Aaron in the priesthood (Numbers 20:23-29). Eleazar's son, Phinehas, was the recipient of a covenant with God granting him and his posterity an "everlasting priesthood" for his part in cleansing Israel of whoredom with other nations (Numbers 25:6-18).

"And thou shalt make holy garments for Aaron thy brother for glory and for beauty" (Exodus 28:2). Aaron was to stand before God for the people as a representative. He must display the holiness and the glory of God. Even his garments had to typify his office. On his head was a gold plate inscribed with the words, "HOLINESS TO THE LORD."

The high priest in the Old Covenant is also a type of Christ. In the Old Covenant, God established priests to mediate between the people and God. They would pray for the people, offer sacrifices, and minister to God on their behalf. Among the priests was a high priest, who would go into the inner sanctuary of the temple once a year to offer an atoning sacrifice for sins. Scripture says that Christ is our high priest—our mediator between us and God. However, unlike regular high priests, he is a perfect priest because he has never sinned and will live forever. Consider the below verses.

> For we have not an high priest which cannot be touched with the feeling of our infirmities; but was in all points tempted like as we are, yet without sin. Let us therefore come boldly unto the throne of grace, that we may obtain mercy, and find grace to help in time of need. (Hebrews 4:15-16)

> For such an high priest became us, who is holy, harmless, undefiled, separate from sinners, and made higher than the heavens; Who needeth not daily, as those high priests, to offer up sacrifice, first for his own sins, and then for the people's: for this he did once, when he offered up himself. (Hebrews 7:26-27)

We do not have space in this work to fully examine Aaron's life and office, nor to consider all the ways he was used of God.

Take Aaron and Eleazar his son, and bring them up unto mount Hor: And strip Aaron of his garments, and put them upon Eleazar his son: and Aaron shall be gathered unto his people, and shall die there. (Numbers 20:25-26)

It was not a good day for Moses and his brother. He was commanded to take Aaron and his son, Eleazar, who would succeed him in the priesthood up to Mount Hor. Aaron's holy garments had to be handed down to his son, so Moses would strip him of them much as a general might strip one in a lower office of their medals.

All men should bring up someone under them to accept the mantle of leadership from their shoulders when their work is done. For Aaron, it was his son, Eleazar.

The brothers had led as the two most powerful men in Israel, the lawmaker and the priest. Their sister had led the women. Memories of the day Moses set the garments upon his brother may have flooded their minds, memories of their meeting at Sinai upon the calling of Moses, memories of them standing before Pharaoh, so many memories.

And Moses did as the LORD commanded: and they went up into mount Hor in the sight of all the congregation. And Moses stripped Aaron of his garments, and put them upon Eleazar his son; and Aaron died there in the top of the mount: and Moses and

Eleazar came down from the mount. (Numbers 20:27-28)

Aaron is the only person in scripture to have the date of their death recorded.

And Aaron the priest went up into mount Hor at the commandment of the LORD, and died there, in the fortieth year after the children of Israel were come out of the land of Egypt, in the first day of the fifth month. (Numbers 33:38)

Aaron's priestly garments were taken and placed upon his son. It was a bittersweet moment. And there Aaron died. Moses and Eleazar returned to the people.

And when all the congregation saw that Aaron was dead, they mourned for Aaron thirty days, even all the house of Israel. (Numbers 20:29)

The usual thirty-day public and solemn mourning period for one of a high position was observed. The entire house of Israel grieved the transition of Aaron, the brother of Moses, called to be the spokesperson for Moses, a prophet in his own right, chosen and attested of God as the first Great High Priest of Israel, and a type and shadow of the priesthood of Christ; a force to be reckoned with, a formidable man.

11 JOSHUA

And if it seem evil unto you to serve the LORD, choose you this day whom ye will serve; whether the gods which your fathers served that were on the other side of the flood, or the gods of the Amorites, in whose land ye dwell: but AS FOR ME AND MY HOUSE, WE WILL SERVE THE LORD. Joshua 14:15.

Joshua, the son of Nun, was a man who was faithful to God in all he did. He assisted Moses in religious matters and in military matters (Exodus 33:11). He was one of the heads of the children of Israel and of the tribe of Ephraim (Numbers 13:8). The name Joshua (Yehoshua or Yeshua in Hebrew) means "Yahveh (also pronounced Yahweh) is deliverance" or "salvation."

We were first introduced to Joshua as Israel journeyed through the wilderness to Rephidim, where there was no water (Exodus 17:1-7). There God provided water when Moses obeyed him in striking the rock in Horeb with the same rod he smote the Red Sea with. The divine presence of God stood upon the rock as he smote it, and pure, refreshing water gushed out of the rock. The Amalekites, a wandering desert tribe, attacked Israel without provocation. Perhaps they wanted to take possession of this valuable water source. The Amalekites were descendants of Esau, Jacob's twin brother; therefore, they were cousins to Israel.

Moses instructed Joshua to choose men to fight with him against Amalek. Moses stood on top of the hill with the rod of God in his hands while they fought. When Moses held his hands up, Israel prevailed in battle; when his hands went down, Amalek prevailed. Aaron and Hur had a stone brought to Moses to sit on, and they held his hands up. God wrought a great victory that day against the Amalekites. "And Joshua discomfited Amalek and his people with the edge of the sword" (Exodus 17:13).

As a military leader, Joshua is undeniably one of the greatest Generals in history. He obeyed God, and God gave him many victories. He was one of the twelve spies sent to report on the Promised Land. Only he and Caleb brought back a report that Israel was able to overcome the inhabitants of the land. He was one of only two Israelites above the age of twenty allowed to enter the Promised Land (Caleb was the other).

Joshua accompanied Moses to Sinai the first time he went to receive the Tablets of Commandments inscribed by God. Joshua was divinely chosen to succeed Moses as the leader of Israel (Numbers 27:15-23).

And the LORD said unto Moses, Take thee Joshua the son of Nun, a man in whom is the spirit, and lay thine hand upon him; And set him before Eleazar the priest, and before all the congregation; and give him a charge in their sight. And thou shalt put some of thine honour upon him, that all the congregation of the children of Israel may be obedient. (Numbers 27:18-20)

Now after the death of Moses the servant of the LORD it came to pass, that the LORD spake unto Joshua the son of Nun, Moses' minister, saying, Moses my servant is dead; now therefore arise, go over this Jordan, thou, and all this people, unto the land which I do give to them, even to the children of Israel. Every place that the sole of your foot shall tread upon, that have I given unto you, as I said unto Moses. From the wilderness and this Lebanon even unto the great river, the river Euphrates, all the land of the Hittites, and unto the great sea toward the going down of the sun, shall be your coast. There shall not any man be able to stand before thee all the days of thy life: as I was with Moses, so I will be with thee: I will not fail thee, nor forsake thee. Be strong and of a good courage: for unto this people shalt thou divide for an inheritance the land, which I sware unto their fathers to give them. (Joshua 1:1-6)

Joshua led Israel in the conquest of Canaan and allocated land to the tribes as he had been given direction. His life is an extraordinary demonstration of faith in God and of godly leadership of a nation and of his family. He was a just man who walked in his integrity. His children and all of Israel were blessed after him. The many ways God used him and the unusual exploits God performed through him during his service under Moses and after he assumed command are too numerous to discuss here.

As a devout father, Joshua was prepared to stand for God, even if he and his family had to stand alone. In his final farewell to Israel, Joshua recalled their history from the call of Abraham, their deliverance from bondage in Egypt, their protection and provision in the wilderness, and their conquest of Canaan. He exhorted them to serve the Lord, who had performed all these mighty works. His example mentored an entire nation in godly leadership.

And it came to pass after these things, that Joshua the son of Nun, the servant of the LORD, died, being an hundred and ten years old. And they buried him in the border of his inheritance in Timnathserah, which is in mount Ephraim, on the north side of the hill of Gaash. **And Israel served the LORD all the days of Joshua, and all the days of the elders that overlived Joshua, and which had known all the works of the LORD, that he had done for Israel**. (Joshua 24:29-31)

Joshua's famous battle cry of, "as for me and my house, we will serve the Lord," can still be heard echoing through the eons of time to challenge all men to lead their households in serving the Lord. He was a force to be reckoned with, a formidable man.

12 CALEB

Now therefore give me this mountain, whereof the LORD spake in that day; for thou heardest in that day how the Anakims were there, and that the cities were great and fenced: if so be the LORD will be with me, then I shall be able to drive them out, as the LORD said. (Joshua 14:12)

Caleb is another great example of a man who demonstrated unconquerable faith in the Lord. He was one of twelve spies sent to view the Promised Land and report to the Children of Israel. He was chosen to represent the tribe of Judah (Numbers 13:6).

The scouts returned from spying on the Promised Land with conflicting reports. Ten thought the giants in the land were too big to fight, but Caleb thought they were too big to miss and urged them to go up at once and take possession of the land "for we are well able to overcome it" (Numbers 13:30).

But the other scouts wimped out, reporting "they are stronger than we" (Numbers 13:31). They said the land devoured its inhabitants, and the men were giants. Caleb knew that the God he served was "well able" to give them victory.

The negative report of ten of the spies caused another rebellion among the people. In opposition to Caleb's report, they caved in, and in their condition of weakness and fear from their recent enslavement, they began to shout and cry out against the Lord and Moses. After all that, they wept like frightened little children all night (Numbers 14:1). Their lack of faith resulted in discontent with the leadership of Moses and Aaron.

The malefactors began murmuring against Moses and Aaron for bringing them out of Egypt, and it created a chain reaction, spreading contagion throughout the congregation. They cried for their children being out in the wilderness instead of in their slave-driven homes in Egypt. As if Pharaoh would welcome them with open arms! Soon, a conspiracy to overthrow the leadership of Moses and Aaron and return to Egypt under the leadership of someone they chose developed, someone who would lead them back into Egypt!

Faith always looks ahead, encouraged by the belief that God will make a way somehow. Unbelief causes us to look back, which often results in complaints because we remember a very different past. Such is the effect of unbelief. Faith looks ahead with courage; unbelief looks back with complaint. Faith unites the people of God; unbelief looks for somebody to blame. There was still time to repent and seek God's face, but the people refused to listen to Caleb and Joshua.

Moses and Aaron fell on their faces before the congregation. Caleb and Joshua tore their clothes to show remorse, grief, mourning, and distress at the lack of faith because they saw what the others did not see: the land's beauty and the power of God to deliver it to them.

Caleb and Joshua told the people the land was good, and if the Lord were pleased with them, he would take them into the land (Numbers 14:7-8). They warned the people not to rebel against God nor fear the people of the land. Caleb and Joshua were the minority among the spies, yet they did not give in, even when the nation turned against them and their lives were in danger. This was an outstanding act of faith and courage. Sometimes you have to stand all alone when you stand for what is right.

Even after this encouragement, the congregation did not repent but thought to stone them. Troubles will inevitably come our way, but when they come, we must trust God all the more, for He is able to deliver us from every evil scheme. Faith ever moves one forward.

The omnipresent God, the great and glorious Being, was invisibly present while Israel conspired against him and his leaders. He always shows up on time. Suddenly, his glory appeared, the Shekinah Glory. His appearance is always a blessing for the faithful but destruction and disaster for the unbeliever and disobedient. Such was the case here. Despite the signs, despite the deliverance from Egyptian tyranny, the miraculous Red Sea crossing, manna from heaven, water from a rock, etc., that Israel had witnessed, they failed to trust in the Lord. God asked how long they would continue to provoke him after all he had done to encourage, protect, defend, and bring them into the land promised their forefathers.

For their unbelief, God struck them with pestilence, a word for plague or death (Numbers 14:12). The ten men who had given the bad report were also struck down and died of a plague before the Lord. But Joshua and Caleb lived because of their great faith. Faith leads to obedience, and unbelief leads to rebellion and death.

God would have deprived all the unbelievers of entering the promised land. Instead, he would have taken Moses and his people and made them an even greater nation in place of this one, but Moses pleaded for forgiveness for the very people who would have stoned him to death if they had their way. God forgave Israel and spared them from immediate judgment. But because of their constant testing of him, none above the age of twenty, except Caleb and Joshua, would be allowed to enter the Promised Land.

> Doubtless ye shall not come into the land, concerning which I sware to make you dwell therein, save Caleb the son of Jephunneh, and Joshua the son of Nun. (Numbers 14:30).

Caleb was singled out as a servant who had a different spirit. He was bold and courageous. He followed God fully and would be rewarded by entering the Promised Land with his descendants. He was also to be rewarded with a lot in the Promised Land for his stupendous acts of faith. In his final words to the nation of Israel, Moses remembered their history and made mention of Caleb and his inheritance in the Promise Land.

Surely there shall not one of these men of this evil generation see that good land, which I sware to give unto your fathers, Save Caleb the son of Jephunneh; he shall see it, and to him will I give the land that he hath trodden upon, and to his children, because he hath wholly followed the LORD. (Deuteronomy 1:35-36)

When they came into the Promise Land, Caleb claimed his inheritance on the day Joshua divided the lots.

And now, behold, the LORD hath kept me alive, as he said, these forty and five years, even since the LORD spake this word unto Moses, while the children of Israel wandered in the wilderness: and now, lo, I am this day fourscore and five years old. As yet I am as strong this day as I was in the day that Moses sent me: as my strength was then, even so is my strength now, for war, both to go out, and to come in. (Joshua 14:10-11)

Caleb was 85 years old on the day Joshua blessed him and divided to him his inheritance in the Promise Land.

Hebron therefore became the inheritance of Caleb the son of Jephunneh the Kenezite unto this day, because that he wholly followed the LORD God of Israel. (Joshua 14:14)

Caleb was as strong on that day as he had been when he went to spy on the land. He was available and ready to continue being used by God. Be a Caleb. Claim your inheritance in the Lord. Like Caleb, you will become a force to be reckoned with, a formidable man.

13 SAMSON

And Samson took hold of the two middle pillars upon which the house stood, and on which it was borne up, of the one with his right hand, and of the other with his left. And Samson said, Let me die with the Philistines. And he bowed himself with all his might; and the house fell upon the lords, and upon all the people that were therein. So the dead which he slew at his death were more than they which he slew in his life. (Judges 16:29-30)

Samson was the last judge of Israel recorded in the Book of Judges, although Samuel was the final judge. Israel sinned, and God delivered them into the hand of the Philistines for forty years. Samson was raised up as a deliverer for his people. His father was Manoah, a man from the tribe of Dan, who lived in Zorah, a city on the boundary of Judah and Dan. Manoah's wife was barren, and they had no children.

And the angel of the LORD appeared unto the woman, and said unto her, Behold now, thou art barren, and bearest not: but thou shalt conceive, and bear a son. Now therefore beware, I pray thee, and drink not wine nor strong drink, and eat not any unclean thing: For, lo, thou shalt conceive, and bear a son; and no razor shall come on his head: for the child shall be a Nazarite unto God from the womb: and he shall begin to deliver Israel out of the hand of the Philistines. (Judges 13:3-5)

Samson was a Nazarite from his mother's womb. A Nazarite was vowed to the Lord, sometimes for a set time and sometimes for their lifetime. Samson was to be a Nazarite all the days of his life. He was not to drink wine or strong liquor, not to eat any unclean thing, and not to cut his hair. He was separated for the work of the Lord. "And the woman bare a son, and called his name Samson: and the child grew, and the LORD blessed him" (Judges 13:24).

Samson met a Philistine woman from Timnath and wanted her as his wife. His mother and father thought he should marry one of his own people. They did not know it was part of God's plan to deliver Israel from the Philistines. Samson went to visit the woman and, on his way, encountered a young lion who came out fiercely against him.

And the Spirit of the LORD came mightily upon him, and he rent him as he would have rent a kid, and he had nothing in his hand: but he told not his father or his mother what he had done. (Judges 14:6)

The Spirit of the Lord endued Samson with supernatural might, and he tore the lion apart as if it had been a small lamb. Samson married the woman and at the feast posed a riddle to thirty young men they had at the feast to be companions to him. If they guessed the riddle within the seven days of the feast, he would give them thirty cloths of linen and thirty change of clothes. If they did not guess, they would have to give him thirty cloths of linen and thirty change of clothes.

The riddle was, "Out of the eater came forth meat, and out of the strong came forth sweetness. And they could not in three days expound the riddle" (Judges 14:14). On his way to the feast, Samson had seen the carcass of the lion he killed before, and bees had made a beehive in it. He found honey in it and bought it to the parents of the woman he was to marry. The men could not guess the riddle and pressured Samson's wife to pressure him for the answer.

On the seventh day, they threatened her with burning her father's house down if she did not get the answer out of Samson. After whining, weeping, and giving him the guilt treatment, Samson was cajoled into giving her the answer on the seventh day. He was physically supernaturally strong but had a weak moral nature for women.

> And the men of the city said unto him on the seventh day before the sun went down, What is sweeter than honey? and what is stronger than a lion? And he said unto them, If ye had not plowed with my heifer, ye had not found out my riddle. (Judges 14:18)

Samson killed thirty men of Askelon and gave their garments to the men who guessed the riddle. He then went to his father's house. While he was at his father's house, the woman was given in marriage to one of the men who had been a companion of his. Sometime later, Samson visited his wife, but her father intercepted him and told him he had given her to his companion. He offered her younger sister in her place. Samson retaliated destructively. He destroyed the crops of the Philistines.

> And Samson went and caught three hundred foxes, and took firebrands, and turned tail to tail, and put a firebrand in the midst between two tails. And when he had set the brands on fire, he let them go into the standing corn of the Philistines, and burnt up both the shocks, and also the standing corn, with the vineyards and olives. (Judges 15:4-5)

The Philistines burned Samson's wife and her father when they found out why Samson had destroyed their crops. Samson avenged himself by killing some, bruising, and breaking the limbs of some others. The Philistines encamped in Judah, intending to capture Samson and punish him. The men of Judah asked why they were coming against them. They told the men of Judah what Samson had done. Three thousand men of Judah went to Mount Etam, where Samson had stationed himself. Samson pretended to be captured. He let them tie his hands and take him to the Philistines.

> And when he came unto Lehi, the Philistines shouted against him: and the Spirit of the LORD came mightily upon him, and the cords that were upon his arms became as flax that was burnt with fire, and his bands loosed from off his hands. (Judges 15:14)

Samson killed a thousand Philistines with the jawbone of a donkey he found. Samson was thirsty after battling the Philistines.

> And he was sore athirst, and called on the LORD, and said, Thou hast given this great deliverance into the hand of thy servant: and now shall I die for thirst, and fall into the hand of the uncircumcised? (Judges 15:18)

He had thrown the jawbone aside, but God made a hollow place in the bone, and water gushed from it. Samson drank the water, and his spirit was refreshed. Twenty years passed with Samson judging all of Israel. One day he traveled to Gaza, a chief city of the Philistines, and went into a harlot that night. Some men from the city hid inside the city gate, intending to kill Samson in the morning.

> And Samson lay till midnight, and arose at midnight, and took the doors of the gate of the city, and the two posts, and went away with them, bar and all, and put them upon his shoulders, and carried them up to the top of an hill that is before Hebron. (Judges 16:3)

At midnight, Samson left, taking the gates, its posts, and its bars with the men hidden inside of it on his shoulders and carrying all of it to a hill near Hebron. Sometime later, Samson fell in love with Delilah, a Philistine woman from the valley of Sorek. The Philistine rulers offered her eleven hundred pieces of silver if she would entice Samson into revealing the source of his strength and tell them. Three times Samson gave her false information concerning where his strength came from. Finally, she used the "if you really love me" guilt trip, and he caved in, revealing that if his hair were cut, he would lose his strength.

> That he told her all his heart, and said unto her, There hath not come a razor upon mine head; for I have been a Nazarite unto God from my mother's womb: if I be shaven, then my strength will go from me, and I shall become weak, and be like any other man. (Judges 16:17)

Delilah called for the rulers of the Philistines and, while Samson slept peacefully with his head on her lap, had them cut his hair off.

> And she said, The Philistines be upon thee, Samson. And he awoke out of his sleep, and said, I will go out as at other times before, and shake myself. And he wist not that the LORD was departed from him. (Judges 16:20)

Too late. He had lain in the wrong arms too many times. You must be careful whom you trust yourself with. Your heart cannot safely trust in everyone. The enemy is watching to entrap you. Samson was taken prisoner, his eyes gauged out, bound, and taken to Gaza to grind grain in the prison house. Samson had lost his immense strength because the spirit of the Lord departed from him when the Nazarite vow was violated.

There are consequences to disobedience, and Samson entrusting himself to a woman who was not a godly woman was disobedience. While the Philistines were rejoicing over capturing Samson and giving praise to their idol gods, while they were mocking the man of God, and while they harbored evil schemes in their hearts, Samson's hair was growing.

> And it came to pass, when their hearts were merry, that they said, Call for Samson, that he may make us sport. And they called for Samson out of the prison house; and he made them sport: and they set him between the pillars. And Samson said unto the lad that held him by the hand, Suffer me that I may feel the pillars whereupon the house standeth, that I may lean upon them. (Judges 16:25-26)

The Philistine rulers were having one of their huge extravaganzas and called for Samson so they could make fun of him. Samson had the young man that led him forth to put his hands on the pillars on each side. The power of the Lord came upon him. He bowed down with all his might, and the house fell in. At his death, Samson killed more Philistines than all he had killed during his lifetime. Samson's relatives came and took him and buried him in the burying place of his father. He is recorded in Hebrews, along with other faithful men and women, as a force to be reckoned with. "And what shall I more say? for the time would fail me to tell of Gedeon, and of Barak, and of Samson, and of Jephthae; of David also, and Samuel, and of the prophets" (Hebrews 11:32). Samson was a force to be reckoned with, a formidable man.

14 SAMUEL

Samuel was a major prophet, a high priest, and the last judge who ruled Israel. He is often cited as the author of the Book of Judges, Ruth, and most of I Samuel.

Samuel's father, Elkanah, had two wives, Peninnah and Hannah. He loved Hannah and treated her well, but she was barren. Hannah prayed for a child in the temple when they went up for the yearly festival that all Jewish males had to attend. She vowed to give the child back to the Lord if he should bless her with one. Eli was priest. He saw her lips moving and thought she was drunk. When she told him she was praying, he prayed that God would grant her petition.

Hannah conceived a son and called his name Samuel ("heard of God" or "name of God"). He was under the Nazarite vow from his mother's womb. That vow states that the person must be separate, he must drink nothing of the vine, and he must not shave his head. Hannah kept her vow. When Samuel was weaned, she took him up to the yearly festival with her husband and placed him in the service of Eli.

> And she said, Oh my lord, as thy soul liveth, my lord, I am the woman that stood by thee here, praying unto the LORD. For this child I prayed; and the LORD hath given me my petition which I asked of him: Therefore also I have lent him to the LORD; as long as he liveth he shall be lent to the LORD. And he worshipped the LORD there. (1 Samuel 1:26-28)

Samuel ministered before the Lord from a child. Hannah entrusted to God what he had entrusted her with, and God blessed her and gave her more children.

> And Eli blessed Elkanah and his wife, and said, The LORD give thee seed of this woman for the loan which is lent to the LORD. And they went unto their own home. And the LORD visited Hannah, so that she conceived, and bare three sons and two daughters. And the child Samuel grew before the LORD. (1 Samuel 2:20-21)

Samuel continued to grow in wisdom and in the knowledge of the Lord. "And Samuel judged Israel all the days of his life" (1 Samuel 7:15).

The voice of the Lord called to Samuel when he was just a child. He ran to Eli, thinking it was him calling. Eli told him to say, "Here am I," the next time the voice called. He did, and the Lord revealed he had told Eli that he would bring an end to his house in the priesthood for the disobedience of his sons. Eli had grown old, and his sons were unfit for the priesthood. God took the priesthood from his sons and set it upon Samuel.

And I will raise me up a faithful priest, that shall do according to that which is in mine heart and in my mind: and I will build him a sure house; and he shall walk before mine anointed for ever. (1 Samuel 2:35)

Samuel had to deliver the message to Eli the next morning, who accepted it.

And Samuel told him every whit, and hid nothing from him. And he said, It is the LORD: let him do what seemeth him good. And Samuel grew, and the LORD was with him, and did let none of his words fall to the ground. (1 Samuel 3:18-19)

The whole of Israel knew Samuel was set to be a prophet for everything that he said came to be. The Philistines attacked Israel, taking the ark of God and killing the sons of Eli. When Eli heard his sons were dead and the ark had been taken, he fell off his seat, breaking his neck, and died.

The wife of Eli's son, Phinehas, went into hard labor when she heard the ark had been taken and her husband and father-in-law were dead. She died giving birth but named the child Ichabod.

And she named the child Ichabod, saying, The glory is departed from Israel: because the ark of God was taken, and because of her father in law and her husband. (1 Samuel 4:21)

The Philistines were troubled by having the ark. Divine judgments fell upon them; disease and loss in battle occurred. They returned the ark with gifts, and it was in Kirjathjearim for twenty years. Samuel called upon Israel to repent before the Lord.

> And they gathered together to Mizpeh, and drew water, and poured it out before the LORD, and fasted on that day, and said there, We have sinned against the LORD. And Samuel judged the children of Israel in Mizpeh. (1 Samuel 7:6)

Under his divinely guided administration, the Philistines were subdued all the days of his rulership. When Samuel was old, he made his sons judges over Israel; but just as Eli's sons did not walk in his integrity, Samuel's sons did not walk in the ways of their father. The people were displeased and demanded that Samuel appoint a king over them. Samuel was against it but took it to the Lord.

> And the LORD said unto Samuel, Hearken unto the voice of the people in all that they say unto thee: for they have not rejected thee, but they have rejected me, that I should not reign over them. (1 Samuel 8:7)

Samuel warned the people that in making a king to rule over them, they would become his subjects. They would be subservient to him. The men would serve in his army, men and women would work in his fields, become cooks in his palace, and a portion of whatever they grew in their fields would become his. But the people persisted. They wanted to be like the world around them.

Nevertheless the people refused to obey the voice of Samuel; and they said, Nay; but we will have a king over us; That we also may be like all the nations; and that our king may judge us, and go out before us, and fight our battles. (1 Samuel 8:19-20)

Samuel yielded to the people and, under God's directions, anointed Saul as king. Saul was the son of Kish, a Benjamite ("a mighty man of power," 1 Samuel 9:1). But Saul was rejected after his sin of offering a burnt offering in the priest's place.

And Samuel said to Saul, Thou hast done foolishly: thou hast not kept the commandment of the LORD thy God, which he commanded thee: for now would the LORD have established thy kingdom upon Israel for ever. But now thy kingdom shall not continue: the LORD hath sought him a man after his own heart, and the LORD hath commanded him to be captain over his people, because thou hast not kept that which the LORD commanded thee. (1 Samuel 13:13-14)

David, the son of Jesse, was anointed in his place, though Saul continued to preside over the government of the Kingdom for awhile more.

And Samuel died; and all the Israelites were gathered together, and lamented him, and buried him in his house at Ramah. And David arose, and went down to the wilderness of Paran. (1 Samuel 25:1)

Samuel, the man of God, the prophet, the priest, and the last judge to reign over Israel, a man born as the answer to his mother's prayer, died. Every mighty man of God must be a prayer warrior. Samuel was conceived as the answer to prayer. He had been nurtured in prayer, brought up in the house of prayer, trained in prayer, and continued in prayer all the days of his life.

Prayer has been taken out of the schools but cannot be taken out of our homes. Make your home a house of prayer. Samuel is named with Moses and Aaron as being among those who prevailed with God in prayer "Moses and Aaron among his priests, and Samuel among them that call upon his name; they called upon the LORD, and he answered them" (Psalms 99:6). He was a force to be reckoned with, a formidable man.

15 DAVID

Then thou spakest in vision to thy holy one, and saidst, I have laid help upon one that is mighty; I have exalted one chosen out of the people. I have found David my servant; with my holy oil have I anointed him: With whom my hand shall be established: mine arm also shall strengthen him. (Psalms 89:19-21)

David was a shepherd, just a young boy tending his father's sheep when he was anointed King in Saul's stead. God chose David, the young shepherd boy, to be king of Israel because he was "a man after his own heart" (1 Samuel 13:14). David was the youngest son of Jesse.

Saul, the first king of Israel, had been rejected because he had acted presumptuously in burning sacrifices himself and disobeyed God in sparing Agag, the king of the Amalekites, when he had been commanded "smite Amalek, and utterly destroy all that they have, and spare them not; but slay both man and woman, infant and suckling, ox and sheep, camel and ass" (1 Samuel 15:3).

He also spared the best of what the Amalekites had.

> And the LORD said unto Samuel, How long wilt thou mourn for Saul, seeing I have rejected him from reigning over Israel? fill thine horn with oil, and go, I will send thee to Jesse the Bethlehemite: for I have provided me a king among his sons. (1 Samuel 16:1)

Samuel, the priest, had been sent to the house of Jesse with divine instructions to anoint another king instead of Saul. After having Jesse's sons pass before him, he still had not seen the Lord's anointed. He asked and was told that Jesse had one other son who tended the sheep, a menial job. He had him brought before him. Never think your job is so menial that God cannot exalt you. Whatever you do, do it to the best of your ability.

> And he sent, and brought him in. Now he was ruddy, and withal of a beautiful countenance, and goodly to look to. And the LORD said, Arise, anoint him: for this is he. Then Samuel took the horn of oil, and anointed him in the midst of his brethren: and the Spirit of the LORD came upon David from that day forward. So Samuel rose up, and went to Ramah. (1 Samuel 16:12-13)

"... the Spirit of the LORD departed from Saul, and an evil spirit from the LORD troubled him" (1 Samuel 16:14). The Kingdom had been taken from Saul and his descendants, but he remained as king for a time. The prophesy against him was troubling. His servants advised him to find a gifted harp player to provide soothing music when the evil spirit came upon him.

Then answered one of the servants, and said, Behold, I have seen a son of Jesse the Bethlehemite, that is cunning in playing, and a mighty valiant man, and a man of war, and prudent in matters, and a comely person, and the LORD is with him. (1 Samuel 16:18)

David was a gifted musician, as well as a gifted singer and writer. He is credited with writing most of the Psalms. The right music ushers us into the presence of the Holy Spirit; it changes the atmosphere. It can remove fears, calm angry tempers, and bring joy and peace to the troubled soul. Whenever David played, "Saul was refreshed, and was well, and the evil spirit departed from him" (1 Samuel 16:23).

There was a standoff between the Philistines and Israel. The Philistines mocked the men of Israel. Goliath was a giant Philistine. He was fearsome in appearance. He stood over nine feet tall. He wore a helmet of brass and metal coats weighing over 150 pounds. He challenged Israel to choose a man to fight against him.

If he be able to fight with me, and to kill me, then will we be your servants: but if I prevail against him, and kill him, then shall ye be our servants, and serve us. And the Philistine said, I defy the armies of Israel this day; give me a man, that we may fight together. (1 Samuel 17:9-10)

Saul and his men quivered in fear. Saul promised the man who would fight and win against Goliath his daughter in marriage, riches, and to free his father's house from having to give part of their crops to the king.

David's father sent him to the battlefield with food supplies for his three oldest brothers, who were in Saul's army, and he learned about the challenge. Like Caleb, who thought the giants in the Promise Land were too big to miss, David thought Goliath could easily be brought down with the Lord on his side.

Saul was hesitant to accept David's offer to fight the Philistine since he was only a youth and Goliath a man of war, but as a shepherd protecting his father's flock, David encountered danger and killed a lion and a bear who stole one of the sheep.

> Thy servant slew both the lion and the bear: and this uncircumcised Philistine shall be as one of them, seeing he hath defied the armies of the living God. David said moreover, The LORD that delivered me out of the paw of the lion, and out of the paw of the bear, he will deliver me out of the hand of this Philistine. And Saul said unto David, Go, and the LORD be with thee. (1 Samuel 17:36-37)

David killed Goliath, the giant, with a slingshot and a pebble because God was with him. God protected and helped David throughout his life.

Saul first honored David, decorating him and giving him his daughter, Michal, as a wife (1 Samuel 18:20–27). Saul became jealous of David when the people began to praise his prowess in battle, causing David to flee from his presence and hide in the wilderness. Saul gave Michal to another man after David fled, but David took her back after he became king.

David assembled a band of mighty men and led raids against the Philistines. His army grew in numbers, and so did his fame. He became a hero among the people. Victory after victory is recorded in the books of Samuel. It was the hand of God that gave David and his men many victories over their enemies.

Saul, and his sons, were killed in a later battle with the Philistines (1 Samuel 31), and David, the anointed one of God, was eventually inaugurated King. The Lord set him into that position because of his faithfulness and promised that his descendants would always rule over Israel. That promise is known as the Davidic Covenant. "And thine house and thy kingdom shall be established for ever before thee: thy throne shall be established for ever" (2 Samuel 7:16).

David sinned against God when he took Bathsheba, the wife of one of his mighty men, in adultery. Uriah was called home from the battle, hoping he would sleep with his wife, who was now pregnant by the king. Uriah would not go home, and David orchestrated his murder by having his commander-in-chief send him to the front lines of the battle. David accepted his sin, and Psalms 51 is his prayer for forgiveness. He sinned against Bathsheba, Uriah, and the general of his army, but his real sin was against God and God alone.

> For I acknowledge my transgressions: and my sin is ever before me. Against thee, thee only, have I sinned, and done this evil in thy sight: that thou mightest be justified when thou speakest, and be clear when thou judgest. (Psalms 51:3-4)

As sovereign ruler, David could not be called into account by any of his subjects. He was anointed and set into this position by God. His military genius, loyalty to his armed forces, and political savvy had won the hearts of his people, united the monarchy, and gained him absolute power.

David had no superior with whom he had to consult before making decisions; neither was there any authority in the land by which he could be judged or condemned. God alone was greater than David, and it was to God alone that he was answerable.

David confessed he had sinned, and God's sentence was righteous, even though it should be the most severe penalty. He did not appeal for leniency or claim his punishment was too much to bear. He just asked to be cleansed. The child Bathsheba birthed died, but she had a second child by David, Solomon, who was the successor to the throne.

David's Mighty Men

These also are the chief of the mighty men whom David had, who strengthened themselves with him in his kingdom, and with all Israel, to make him king, according to the word of the LORD concerning Israel. (1 Chronicles 11:10)

As part of his last words, David remembered and commended the captains who had served under his command. The mighty Joab is not mentioned, but he served as commander-in-chief of the armed forces. He was the son of David's sister, Zeruiah.

The list in 2 Samuel 23 has to be reconciled with the list in 1 Chronicles 11 for a better understanding. The names listed may include the names of captains who died in battle and those appointed in their stead. The first and greatest of David's mighty men were Jashobeam, Eleazar, and Shammah. Jashobeam the Tachmonite, chief of the captains, slew three hundred men at one time according to 1 Chronicles 11:11; and eight hundred according to 2 Samuel 23:8.

Eleazar was with David when the Philistines attacked once, and the men of Israel fled.

He arose, and smote the Philistines until his hand was weary, and his hand clave unto the sword: and the LORD wrought a great victory that day; and the people returned after him only to spoil. (2 Samuel 23:10)

The third of the three mightiest men was Shammah, who defended a piece of ground when the people fled from the Philistines. "But he stood in the midst of the ground, and defended it, and slew the Philistines: and the LORD wrought a great victory" (2 Samuel 23:12).

The next three mighty men did mighty exploits also, but did not attain to the degree of the first three.

Abishai, the brother of Joab, "was chief of the three: for lifting up his spear against three hundred, he slew them, and had a name among the three" (2 Samuel 23:18, 1 Chronicles 11:20).

Benaiah was set over the personal guard of David. He "slew two lionlike men of Moab: he went down also and slew a lion in the midst of a pit in time of snow: And he slew an Egyptian, a goodly man: and the Egyptian had a spear in his hand; but he went down to him with a staff, and plucked the spear out of the Egyptian's hand, and slew him with his own spear" (2 Samuel 23:20-21). Many other valiant warriors of the great armies of David are listed.

The most well-known feat of heroism performed by three of David's mighty men is breaking through enemy lines to get David a drink of water which he longed for from the well of Bethlehem.

And the three mighty men brake through the host of the Philistines, and drew water out of the well of Bethlehem, that was by the gate, and took it, and brought it to David: nevertheless he would not drink thereof, but poured it out unto the LORD. And he said, Be it far from me, O LORD, that I should do this: is not this the blood of the men that went in jeopardy of their lives? therefore he would not drink it. These things did these three mighty men. (2 Samuel 23:16-17)

David poured the water out before the Lord as a drink offering, for he valued his soldiers' sacrifice in risking their lives for their Chief.

The Temple

Then David the king stood up upon his feet, and said, Hear me, my brethren, and my people: As for me, I had in mine heart to build an house of rest for the ark of the

covenant of the LORD, and for the footstool of our God, and had made ready for the building: But God said unto me, Thou shalt not build an house for my name, because thou hast been a man of war, and hast shed blood.
(1 Chronicles 28:2-3 KJV)

David attempted to bring the Ark of the Covenant from Kirjathjearim to the City of David (Jerusalem). His first attempt resulted in the death of one of the men carrying it when he reached out to steady it. The ark was carried into the house of Obed-Edom the Gittite (1 Samuel 6:10). After three months; he made another attempt to bring the ark to Jerusalem, which was successful.

It was in David's heart to build a temple for the Lord. He was given the blueprints for the temple but was not allowed to build it. Instead, he had to pass them to his successor. Even as God showed Moses the pattern for the Tabernacle in the wilderness, so David was given the details of the plan for the temple by inspiration and wrote them down from the hand of the Lord.

Although David was not permitted to build the house of the Lord, he nevertheless spent years preparing for it with all his abilities and all of his might. The temple that came to be known as Solomon's Temple was not built for him or even for David – "and the work is great: for the palace is not for man, but for the LORD God" (1 Chronicles 29:1). The work was great because it was for the glory of the Lord and, therefore, magnificent.

Solomon rose to the throne on the shoulders of his father, becoming the first in the accession of the Davidic

Covenant, of whom his father was the recipient. David had prepared for the building of the temple before his death, providing abundant materials and resources and, most importantly, the blueprint handed down from the Lord to him.

Solomon continued to add to the materials and resources during the first years of his reign, and in the fourth year, the actual work commenced. The entire process took seven and a half years.

The temple was prayerfully dedicated amidst innumerable sacrifices and lavish thanksgiving in what is perhaps the grandest ceremony ever performed under the Mosaic dispensation. The edifice was most luxurious and full of splendor, yet it could not compare with the glory of God manifested as a seal of divine approval. Solomon's execution of God's instructions for the house of the Lord exemplifies excellence in the kingdom.

After the dedication of the great temple, God appeared to Solomon and told him that if the people called by his name should forsake him and sin, they would suffer the consequences of his judgment. He also promised to hear and answer the prayers of his people made in the temple by removing the judgment, but action would be required on their part.

The Tabernacle, the temple, and the priestly services performed in them were merely types and shadows of heavenly things to be continued until they were fulfilled in Christ. So then we acknowledge the obedience of David and Solomon in building this great architectural masterpiece, but the glory belongs to God.

As his chosen people, we have a greater temple than Solomon's. We have the true temple, the Lord Jesus Christ, and his blood shed for the remission of sins. Yesterday is forever past; tomorrow may not arrive. All you really have is this moment. Serve the Lord with all of your heart, with all of your soul, with all of your strength, with all of your might.

Now the acts of David the king, first and last, behold, they are written in the book of Samuel the seer, and in the book of Nathan the prophet, and in the book of Gad the seer, With all his reign and his might, and the times that went over him, and over Israel, and over all the kingdoms of the countries. (1 Chronicles 29:29-30)

David – the son of Jesse, the grandson of Obed, the great-grandson of Boaz and Ruth, the shepherd boy, the giant killer, the valiant warrior, the man who was raised up on high, the greatest monarch on earth, the anointed of the God of Jacob, the sweet psalmist of Israel, a man after God's own heart – "died in a good old age, full of days, riches, and honour" (1 Chronicles 29:28), having done all that was assigned into his mighty hands. He was a force to be reckoned with, a formidable man.

16 ELIJAH

And Elijah the Tishbite, who was of the inhabitants of Gilead, said unto Ahab, As the LORD God of Israel liveth, before whom I stand, there shall not be dew nor rain these years, but according to my word.
(1 Kings 17:1)

Elijah the Tishbite, one of the most eminent prophets in the Bible, emerged abruptly on the stage of history. We know nothing of Elijah before this point. Like Melchizedek, he seems to have no beginning, and because he did not suffer death, he seems to have no end. Scripture is silent concerning his birth and his parents. His name means "My God is Yahvey (or Yahweh)."

Elijah bravely confronted King Ahab to deliver the message that a drought was coming. The Bible says the same thing about King Ahab that it said of his father, Omri, before him; he "did evil in the sight of the LORD above all that were before him" (1 Kings 16:30). Ahab married Jezebel, the daughter of Ethbaal, King of the Zidonians. They worshipped the idol god Baal, and Ahab committed apostasy by converting to worship him also.

> And he reared up an altar for Baal in the house of Baal, which he had built in Samaria. And Ahab made a grove; and Ahab did more to provoke the LORD God of Israel to anger than all the kings of Israel that were before him. (1 Kings 16:32-33)

Ahab was weak-willed, and Jezebel ruled over him and the realm. "But there was none like unto Ahab, which did sell himself to work wickedness in the sight of the LORD, whom Jezebel his wife stirred up" (1 Kings 21:25). Jezebel was relentlessly cruel to the people of God, persecuting true believers and putting to death many of the prophets and priests. At this crucial junction, Elijah suddenly surfaced and delivered the message of judgment against Israel.

> And the word of the LORD came unto him, saying, Get thee hence, and turn thee eastward, and hide thyself by the brook Cherith, that is before Jordan. And it shall be, that thou shalt drink of the brook; and I have commanded the ravens to feed thee there. (1 Kings 17:2-4)

After hearing the message, Ahab would certainly tell Jezebel the real power in Israel, and she would seek the life of Elijah. Those whom God sends, he also protects, and he hid Elijah by the brook Cherith, which flows into the Jordan River. In God, you will find a hiding place in the time of trial. He is a strong shelter in the time of storm. No matter the problem, no matter the struggle, there is a Cherith for you.

Elijah's food was delivered twice a day by ravens: bread and meat in the mornings and the evenings, and he drank from the brook Cherith. The drought lasted three years and six months (1 Kings 18:1, Luke 4:25, James 5:17-18). In time, Cherith dried up, but God had a plan. If your brook has run dry, if your future seems to be on hold, if your mountains are high and your valleys low, remember that God always has a plan for you.

God commanded Elijah to go to Zarephath, a city near Zidon, the very place where Jezebel was born. Zidon means "hunting," but Jezebel would probably never hunt for Elijah so close to her hometown. He would be hidden in plain view. Elijah was sent to a widow's home, where he would be sustained. We only know this woman as the Widow of Zarephath.

She was a widow living in poverty with her child. The drought had taken a devastating toll on the land. She only had a small amount of meal and oil left. She was gathering sticks to make one last meal for her and her son when Elijah arrived. Approaching the city gates, he saw the woman gathering sticks and knew by divine revelation that she was the woman whom God had chosen to sustain him.

Elijah asked the woman for water and, as she was going to fetch it, asked her to bring him a morsel of bread also. He gave her a promise that if she did as he asked, all would be well. Though her situation was desperate, at his word, the woman did as Elijah said, making a little cake for him first. "The barrel of meal shall not waste, neither shall the cruse of oil fail, until the day that the LORD sendeth rain upon the earth" (1 Kings 17:14).

And she went and did according to the saying of Elijah: and she, and he, and her house, did eat many days. And the barrel of meal wasted not, neither did the cruse of oil fail, according to the word of the LORD, which he spake by Elijah. (1 Kings 17:15-16)

The widow of Zarephath was rewarded with meal and oil throughout the remaining drought for her remarkable act. She was not even an Israelite, but she and her household lived and flourished just because she obeyed the man of God.

Sometime later, the same woman's son fell ill and died. Elijah took her son from her bosom, carried him up to the loft, and laid him on his bed. He prayed, stretching himself upon the child three times and calling upon the Lord to let his soul return to him again. God heard Elijah's cry, and the child's soul returned, and he was brought back to life. It is the first recorded instance in the Bible of a man being raised from the dead.

And Elijah took the child, and brought him down out of the chamber into the house, and delivered him unto his mother: and Elijah said, See, thy son liveth. And the woman said to Elijah, Now by this I know that thou art a man of God, and that the word of the LORD in thy mouth is truth. (1 Kings 17:23-24)

What joy this mother must have experienced to have her son raised from the dead! Now, the widow had gained more than food and sustenance. She had gained confirmation that Elijah was indeed a man of God and that his words were true. "Jesus said unto her, I am the resurrection, and the life: he that believeth in me, though he were dead, yet shall he live: And whosoever liveth and believeth in me shall never die. Believest thou this?" (John 11:25-26.)

The word Zarephath means "refinery." Refining is removing the impurities so that the end product is pure, free of imperfection. Elijah was sent to Zarephath to be refined for his mission to speak before kings on behalf of the Lord. The widow of Zarephath was being refined by her trials to be used of God. Your trials are the process you go through to be made fit for the kingdom. You are being refined! You shall come forth as pure gold!

> And it came to pass after many days, that the word of the LORD came to Elijah in the third year, saying, Go, shew thyself unto Ahab; and I will send rain upon the earth. (1 Kings 18:1)

Elijah moved at God's command. He was commanded to tell Ahab that rain was coming in the third year of the drought. Ahab, and his chief steward, Obadiah, were looking for a water source to save the livestock. Obadiah was a man who feared the Lord. He had hidden 100 of the prophets of God when Jezebel was having them killed off inside two caves and fed them with bread and water.

Obadiah saw Elijah and recognized him. He immediately fell on his face in respect for the man of God. Those who recognize the God in others will be blessed. Elijah solicited him to tell Ahab he was there and assured him he would not disappear while Obadiah went to get the king.

And it came to pass, when Ahab saw Elijah, that Ahab said unto him, Art thou he that troubleth Israel? And he answered, I have not troubled Israel; but thou, and thy father's house, in that ye have forsaken the commandments of the LORD, and thou hast followed Baalim. (1 Kings 18:17-18)

Face to face with Ahab, Elijah told him what the real trouble was in Israel; he had forsaken the commandments of the Lord and served Baal. He ordered him to gather all the rulers of Israel and the prophets of Baal to Mount Carmel for a showdown. At Mount Carmel, Elijah called for Israel to return to the Lord.

And call ye on the name of your gods, and I will call on the name of the LORD: and the God that answereth by fire, let him be God. And all the people answered and said, It is well spoken. (1 Kings 18:24)

The prophets of Baal cut a bullock, placed it on the altar, and prayed for fire but were not answered. Elijah mocked them for their efforts. They jumped on the altar, cut themselves, and cried aloud for hours, but to no avail.

Elijah repaired the altar of the Lord, which had been broken. He took twelve stones, one for each of the twelve tribes of Israel, and built an altar to the Lord. He cut a bullock into four pieces and laid it on the altar's wood. Four buckets of water were poured over the animal and the wood. Then another four buckets were poured over the sacrifice. It was done a third time. The trench around the altar was also filled with water. There would be no doubt of the divine source of the fire.

Elijah prayed to the "Lord God of Abraham, Isaac, and of Israel" (1 Kings 18:36).

> Then the fire of the LORD fell, and consumed the burnt sacrifice, and the wood, and the stones, and the dust, and licked up the water that was in the trench. And when all the people saw it, they fell on their faces: and they said, The LORD, he is the God; the LORD, he is the God. (1 Kings 18:38-39)

After this monumental miracle, the prophets of Baal were slain by the Israelites, who returned to the Lord. Elijah told Ahab to return home because an abundant rain would fall. Elijah bowed to the ground with his head between his knees and sent his servant to go up and look toward the sea. The servant went seven times, and on the seventh time, he saw a small cloud rising from the sea in the shape of a man's hand. He told his servant to tell Ahab to prepare his chariot and get from the mountain so he wouldn't be caught in the rain.

> And it came to pass in the mean while, that the heaven was black with clouds and wind, and there was a great rain. And Ahab rode, and went to Jezreel. And the hand of the LORD was on Elijah; and he girded up his loins, and ran before Ahab to the entrance of Jezreel. (1 Kings 18:45-46)

Ahab told Jezebel what Elijah had done and how her prophets had been slain, which sent her into a fury.

> Then Jezebel sent a messenger unto Elijah, saying, So let the gods do to me, and more also, if I make not thy

life as the life of one of them by to morrow about this time. (1 Kings 19:2)

Elijah fled for his life. He went to Beersheba, a providence in Judah, and left his servant there. He left Beersheba and traveled for a day in the wilderness. Sitting under a juniper tree, he asked God to let him die. After every great success, most leaders suffer disappointment. Elijah was disappointed. He felt he had done all he could in the service of the Lord. Know that when you have done all you can, you are at the right place for God to give you a rest so you might have the strength to go on to the next mission.

There in the crucibles of his misery, God nourished Elijah. An angel brought him food, and he rested. The angel brought him food the second time and told him to "Arise and eat; because the journey is too great for thee" (1 Kings 19:7). In those times when God is nourishing you, it is to energize you for the journey ahead. Your work is not done. God is not finished using you for his glory.

Elijah traveled forty days and forty nights on the strength of the food from heaven to Mount Horeb. Moses fasted on Mount Horeb forty days each time he went to receive the Tablets of Commandments. Christ fasted forty days in the wilderness. A forty-day fast without any food or water can only be undertaken by supernatural means.

Elijah took shelter in a cave on Mount Horeb, and God visited him there. When God asked him what he was doing there, he responded that Israel had fallen into apostasy, thrown down his altars, and slain his prophets. He was the only one left to defend the name of the Lord, and they were seeking to take his life. This sentiment of one feeling they're the only one left has been referred to as the "Elijah Complex."

God sent Elijah back to work. He was to anoint Hazael king over Syria (1 Kings 19:15). He was to anoint Jehu king over Israel, and Elisha, the son of Shaphat, to succeed him as the chief prophet in his stead (1 Kings 19:16).

And it shall come to pass, that him that escapeth the sword of Hazael shall Jehu slay: and him that escapeth from the sword of Jehu shall Elisha slay. Yet I have left me seven thousand in Israel, all the knees which have not bowed unto Baal, and every mouth which hath not kissed him. (1 Kings 19:17-18)

God will never leave himself without a man or woman to carry on the work of the Kingdom. Elijah was not the only one, and you are not the only one. Finding Elisha plowing in his father's fields, Elijah threw his mantle upon him. This symbolized the transference of the power of the prophetic office from Elijah to Elisha. After preparing a meal for his family, Elisha bid them farewell and followed Elijah.

It was not Elijah's time to retire yet. He was left to continue the work and mentor Elisha for a while more. He opposed the horrible death of Naboth whose land Ahab coveted. Through the evil scheme of Jezebel, Ahab could took possession of the land (1 Kings 21:17–29). Elijah was sent to deliver a message that his Kingdom was finished and what his end would be.

Behold, I will bring evil upon thee, and will take away thy posterity, and will cut off from Ahab him that pisseth against the wall, and him that is shut up and left in Israel, And will make thine house like the house of Jeroboam the son of Nebat, and like the house of Baasha the son of Ahijah, for the provocation wherewith thou hast provoked me to anger, and made Israel to sin. And of Jezebel also spake the LORD, saying, The dogs shall eat Jezebel by the wall of Jezreel. Him that dieth of Ahab in the city the dogs shall eat; and him that dieth in the field shall the fowls of the air eat. (1 Kings 21:21-24)

Ahab repented when confronted with this prophecy by fasting and laying in sackcloth. God heard his prayers and spared him from seeing his kingdom destroyed. Will God hear the prayers of the wicked? Yes, if they truly repent and seek his face.

Seest thou how Ahab humbleth himself before me? because he humbleth himself before me, I will not bring the evil in his days: but in his son's days will I bring the evil upon his house. (1 Kings 21:29)

Ahaziah, the Samaritan King, fell and suffered a grievous injury. He sent servants to inquire of the idol god of Ekron, Baalzebub, whether he would recover. God commanded Elijah to meet the messengers and ask why he would inquire from the God of Ekron.

Now therefore thus saith the LORD, Thou shalt not come down from that bed on which thou art gone up, but shalt surely die. And Elijah departed. (2 Kings 1:4)

When his servants bought him the message and identified the messenger, Ahaziah sent one of his captains with fifty men after him. Elijah called down fire from heaven, and they were consumed. He sent another captain and fifty more men. Fire also rained from heaven and consumed them. But the third captain prayed that his life and his men be spared, and an angel told Elijah not to be afraid but go with the man. Elijah delivered the message to the king. Because he had inquired of the idol god and not the Lord God of Israel, he would surely die. And Ahaziah died as Elijah had spoken.

> And it came to pass, when the LORD would take up Elijah into heaven by a whirlwind, that Elijah went with Elisha from Gilgal. And Elijah said unto Elisha, Tarry here, I pray thee; for the LORD hath sent me to Bethel. And Elisha said unto him, As the LORD liveth, and as thy soul liveth, I will not leave thee. So they went down to Bethel. (2 Kings 2:1-2)

Elijah's translation is unique in Bible history. It is incomparable. It is a powerful demonstration of how God retires his servants in glory. There is only one other man who did not see death, Enoch. Elisha knew the Lord would translate Elijah and refused to leave him. They went from Gilgal to Bethel, from Bethel to Jericho, and from Jericho to the Jordan River. Other prophets kept telling Elisha that God would take Elijah that day, but Elisha already knew. Fifty prophets stood far off from Elisha and Elijah to witness his homegoing.

> And Elijah took his mantle, and wrapped it together, and smote the waters, and they were divided hither and

thither, so that they two went over on dry ground. (2 Kings 2:8)

Elijah's final miracle was to divide the waters of the Jordan so that he and Elisha could cross on dry ground. On the other side, he gave Elisha a final opportunity to ask for a blessing from him. Elisha asked that a double portion of his prophetic spirit be conferred upon him. The eldest son of a Hebrew received a double portion of the inheritance, and Elisha had already been appointed as the successor to Elijah. He, therefore, asked for a double portion of his spirit.

Elijah told him he had asked a hard thing, but it would be given if he saw him being taken up. He would not receive the double portion if he did not see him being taken up. Young men, if you aspire to greatness, keep your eyes on the Lord and follow after the manner of those who have been anointed of him.

And it came to pass, as they still went on, and talked, that, behold, there appeared a chariot of fire, and horses of fire, and parted them both asunder; and Elijah went up by a whirlwind into heaven. And Elisha saw it, and he cried, My father, my father, the chariot of Israel, and the horsemen thereof. And he saw him no more: and he took hold of his own clothes, and rent them in two pieces. He took up also the mantle of Elijah that fell from him, and went back, and stood by the bank of Jordan; And he took the mantle of Elijah that fell from him, and smote the waters, and said, Where is the LORD God of Elijah? and when he also had smitten the waters, they parted hither and thither: and Elisha went over. (2 Kings 2:11-14)

Elisha did not take his eyes off Elijah and, therefore, was allowed to see his translation. There are no words to describe this awesome, unparalleled event! "The chariot of Israel and the horsemen thereof!" Because he watched the man of God intently, he received a double portion of his prophetic spirit. He took up the mantle of Elijah and parted the waters so that he walked back to the other side of Jordan alone on dry ground. He was without his spiritual father, but he had a double portion of his power in the Lord and went on to do great things to advance the Kingdom.

Elijah and Moses appeared with Jesus on the Mount of Transfiguration.

And after six days Jesus taketh Peter, James, and John his brother, and bringeth them up into an high mountain apart, And was transfigured before them: and his face did shine as the sun, and his raiment was white as the light. And, behold, there appeared unto them Moses and Elias talking with him. (Matthew 17:1-3)

Some scholars speculate that Moses and Elijah are the two faithful witnesses in Revelation during the end times.

And I will give power unto my two witnesses, and they shall prophesy a thousand two hundred and threescore days, clothed in sackcloth. These are the two olive trees, and the two candlesticks standing before the God of the earth. (Revelation 11:3-4)

Some speculate Elijah and Enoch are these two witnesses because they did not see death. There are many other speculations as to who these two powerful witnesses might be, but this is not the place for that discussion.

So then Elijah – the man of God, the seer, the preeminent prophet of his day, the messenger of the Lord, one whom God fed at the hands of an angel and by ravens, the man who was the first in the Bible to raise someone from the dead, the man who prayed and the heavens shut themselves up, the man who called fire down from heaven on the heads of his enemies, the man bold enough to stand before kings and tell them their kingdom was ended – did not see death. His departure was as sudden and dramatic as his entrance into Bible history. He was lifted by a whirlwind from earth to glory. Elijah was a force to be reckoned with, a formidable man.

17 JONADAB

And when he was departed thence, he lighted on Jehonadab the son of Rechab coming to meet him: and he saluted him, and said to him, Is thine heart right, as my heart is with thy heart? And Jehonadab answered, It is. If it be, give me thine hand. And he gave him his hand; and he took him up to him into the chariot.
(2 Kings 10:15)

Jonadab (or Jehonadab), the Rechabite (Hebrew *yonadab* or *yehonadab*, meaning "God is generous" or "noble" or "God has impelled)," is a spectacular example of a righteous man who passed on his faithfulness to successive generations after him.

He was descended from the Kenites, the family of Moses' father-in-law, Jethro.

And the children of the Kenite, Moses' father in law, went up out of the city of palm trees with the children of Judah into the wilderness of Judah, which lieth in the south of Arad; and they went and dwelt among the people. (Judges 1:16)

And the families of the scribes which dwelt at Jabez; the Tirathites, the Shimeathites, and Suchathites. These are the Kenites that came of Hemath, the father of the house of Rechab. (1 Chronicles 2:55)

Jonadab supported Jehu in destroying the house of Ahab and his wife, Jezebel, and in suppressing the worship of Baal after the time of Ahab around 841 BC (2 Kings Chapters 9-10). He rode with Jehu in his chariot to Samaria to slay all that remained of Ahab's family.

And he said, Come with me, and see my zeal for the LORD. So they made him ride in his chariot. And when he came to Samaria, he slew all that remained unto Ahab in Samaria, till he had destroyed him, according to the saying of the LORD, which he spake to Elijah. (2 Kings 10:16-17)

And Jehu went, and Jehonadab the son of Rechab, into the house of Baal, and said unto the worshippers of Baal, Search, and look that there be here with you none of the servants of the LORD, but the worshippers of Baal only. (2 Kings 10:23)

Jonadab commanded his children and their descendants not to drink wine or build houses but to live in tents. They were not to plant crops or vineyards. He promised his descendants that if they obeyed these commands, they would live long, prosperous lives in the land where they were strangers. His promise was based on the principle of the fifth commandment. "Honour thy father and thy mother: that thy days may be long upon the land which the LORD thy God giveth thee" (Exodus 20:12).

Some 250 years later, God tested the Rechabite's obedience to Jonadab's commands to condemn the disobedience of the Jews to God, their father. God told Jeremiah to bring the Rechabites into one of the chambers in the house of the Lord and offer them wine (Jeremiah 35:1-2).

The test was conducted publicly, so there might be witnesses. Jeremiah brought all the chiefs of the Rechabite clan into the chamber of the sons of Hanan, a man of God. It was near the chambers of the princes, which were above the chamber of the doorkeeper. Jeremiah set pots of wine and cups before them and told them to drink the wine (Jeremiah 35:3-5), to which they strongly refused without hesitation.

The wine was offered but not commanded in the name of the Lord. They would most likely have obeyed a command in the name of the Lord. The point of this test was not to persuade them to drink wine publicly but to display their steadfast obedience to their father's commands.

> But they said, We will drink no wine: for Jonadab the son of Rechab our father commanded us, saying, Ye shall drink no wine, neither ye, nor your sons for ever: Neither shall ye build house, nor sow seed, nor plant vineyard, nor have any: but all your days ye shall dwell in tents; that ye may live many days in the land where

ye be strangers. Thus have we obeyed the voice of Jonadab the son of Rechab our father in all that he hath charged us, to drink no wine all our days, we, our wives, our sons, nor our daughters; Nor to build houses for us to dwell in: neither have we vineyard, nor field, nor seed: But we have dwelt in tents, and have obeyed, and done according to all that Jonadab our father commanded us. But it came to pass, when Nebuchadrezzar king of Babylon came up into the land, that we said, Come, and let us go to Jerusalem for fear of the army of the Chaldeans, and for fear of the army of the Syrians: so we dwell at Jerusalem. (Jeremiah 35:6-11)

The Rechabites could say they had obeyed the voice of their father in all he had charged them. They had not drunk wine, built houses, or planted vineyards. They had lived in tents. They were a nomadic people. It was only because Nebuchadnezzar had laid siege to Israel that they came to stay at Jerusalem.

The obedience of the Rechabites resulted in a sharp rebuke and warning for the people of God. They had faithfully obeyed their earthly father's commands, but Israel had not kept their heavenly father's commands. He had sent prophets to warn them, yet they continued to be led astray.

Thus saith the LORD of hosts, the God of Israel; Go and tell the men of Judah and the inhabitants of Jerusalem, Will ye not receive instruction to hearken to my words? saith the LORD. The words of Jonadab the son of Rechab, that he commanded his sons not to drink wine, are performed; for unto this day they drink none, but obey their father's commandment: notwithstanding I have spoken unto you, rising early and speaking; but ye hearkened not unto me. I have sent also unto you all my servants the prophets, rising up early and sending them, saying, Return ye now every man from his evil way, and amend your doings, and go not after other gods to serve them, and ye shall dwell in the land which I have given to you and to your fathers: but ye have not inclined your ear, nor hearkened unto me. (Jeremiah 35:13-15)

God had graciously forgiven Israel time after time. The United Monarchy of Israel had split under Solomon's son, Rehoboam, about 930 B.C. Ten tribes formed the independent Kingdom of Israel in the north. Judah and Benjamin remained under the Davidic Kingdom of Judah in the south. The Assyrian Empire had captured the northern kingdom of Israel around 722 B.C.

Jeremiah warned Judah to repent of their evil ways and turn from other gods, but they had not obeyed him. They had repeatedly been unfaithful. In contrast, Jonadab's descendants had been faithful to the statutes of their father for centuries. Because of their repeated failures of obedience, God would remove his protection from Judah. The city would be destroyed, and they would be carried away captive. The Babylonian Empire destroyed the city in 586 B.C.

Because the sons of Jonadab the son of Rechab have performed the commandment of their father, which he commanded them; but this people hath not hearkened unto me: Therefore thus saith the LORD God of hosts, the God of Israel; Behold, I will bring upon Judah and upon all the inhabitants of Jerusalem all the evil that I have pronounced against them: because I have spoken unto them, but they have not heard; and I have called unto them, but they have not answered. (Jeremiah 35:16-17)

The Rechabites were commended for their unwavering obedience in keeping their father's precepts.

And Jeremiah said unto the house of the Rechabites, Thus saith the LORD of hosts, the God of Israel; Because ye have obeyed the commandment of Jonadab your father, and kept all his precepts, and done according unto all that he hath commanded you: Therefore thus saith the LORD of hosts, the God of Israel; Jonadab the son of Rechab shall not want a man to stand before me for ever. (Jeremiah 35:18-19)

The extraordinary model of obedience exhibited by the Rechabites was a complete reversal of the refusal to receive instruction among the people of Judah. Obedience to parents is obedience to God. It brings him glory, and God rewards those that bring him glory. Because his descendants had obeyed the commandment of Jonadab, God honored them with the promise that "Jonadab the son of Rechab" would not ""lack a man to stand before Me forever." The descendants of this amazing earthly father would have a special standing before their eternal Father forever.

18 JOB

There was a man in the land of Uz, whose name was Job; and that man was perfect and upright, and one that feared God, and eschewed evil. (Job 1:1)

Job. Consider, for a moment, the "man in the land of Uz, whose name was Job" as an example of a righteous man, a devoted husband, and a devout father (Job 1:1). The Bible's first information about Job is that he lived in the land of Uz. Some scholars place the land of Uz in Northern Arabia. Over the years, the expression "land of Uz" was applied to a broader area of land to the south and east of Israel, including Edom, Moab, and Ammon. Jeremiah mentions this land in a warning from the Lord to Judah.

> To wit, Jerusalem, and the cities of Judah, and the kings thereof, and the princes thereof, to make them a desolation, an astonishment, an hissing, and a curse; as it is this day; Pharaoh king of Egypt, and his servants, and his princes, and all his people; And all the mingled people, and all the kings of the land

of Uz, and all the kings of the land of the Philistines, and Ashkelon, and Azzah, and Ekron, and the remnant of Ashdod, Edom, and Moab, and the children of Ammon. (Jeremiah 25:18-21)

Jeremiah places Edom in the land of Uz in Lamentations.

Rejoice and be glad, O daughter of Edom, that dwellest in the land of Uz; the cup also shall pass through unto thee: thou shalt be drunken, and shalt make thyself naked. (Lamentations 4:21)

Job was "perfect and upright," that is, he reverenced the Lord and obeyed his commandments. He "eschewed" or turned away from evil.

Job had an abundance of everything. He was blessed with "seven sons and three daughters" and excessive material wealth (Job 1:2).

His substance also was seven thousand sheep, and three thousand camels, and five hundred yoke of oxen, and five hundred she asses, and a very great household; so that this man was the greatest of all the men of the east. (Job 1:3)

Of all the men, kings, and rulers of the East, Job was the greatest. His wealth far surpassed that of others. No one came close to having as much property, livestock, silver, and gold as Job. When he came to the gates of the city, young men hurriedly stood at a respectful distance, and the older men listened for him to speak.

Moreover, Job was a virtuous man concerned for his children's welfare and their relationship with God. Job's children clearly enjoyed one another's company and came together for feasts, probably to celebrate special days such as birthdays. After their feasting days, Job sent for them and sanctified them by rising early in the morning and offering burnt offerings for each of them. "It may be that my sons have sinned, and cursed God in their hearts. Thus did Job continually" (Job 1:5). So, Job taught his children to honor the Lord. to examine their own conscience, and repent of any sin they may have committed knowingly or unknowingly. What we need today is more men like Job, who will lead their families in the way of righteousness.

Job was a very wise, a man of renown who garnered the highest respect from those who knew him. His reputation was spotless. People sought his counsel. His decisions were the final word on a matter.

> Unto me men gave ear, and waited, and kept silence at my counsel. After my words they spake not again; and my speech dropped upon them. And they waited for me as for the rain; and they opened their mouth wide as for the latter rain. If I laughed on them, they believed it not; and the light of my countenance they cast not down. I chose out their way, and sat chief, and dwelt as a king in the army, as one that comforteth the mourners. (Job 29:21-25)

Some have put forth the theory that Job was a fictional character and that no concrete facts identify him in history. However, the first chapter and the latter part of the final chapter of the Book of Job reveal much historical evidence. That Job was a real person is substantiated by scripture. God attests to his being a real person when he uses him, along with Noah and Daniel, as examples of righteousness to deliver a warning to Jerusalem of impending judgment because of their immorality through the prophet Ezekiel.

> Though these three men, Noah, Daniel, and Job, were in it, they should deliver but their own souls by their righteousness, saith the Lord GOD. (Ezekiel 14:14)

James attests to Job as being a real person and counts him among the prophets.

> Take, my brethren, the prophets, who have spoken in the name of the Lord, for an example of suffering affliction, and of patience. Behold, we count them happy which endure. Ye have heard of the patience of Job, and have seen the end of the Lord; that the Lord is very pitiful, and of tender mercy. (James 5:10-11)

Job had the highest praise a man can receive. God held him up before Satan as an example of righteousness. Satan said it was not for nothing that Job feared God. God was a shield all around Job, and had blessed him above all men. Why shouldn't he walk in righteousness?

> Hast not thou made an hedge about him, and about his house, and about all that he hath on every side? thou hast blessed the work of his hands, and his substance is increased in the land. But put forth thine hand now, and touch all that he hath, and he will curse thee to thy face. (Job 1:10-11)

To prove Job's faith, God allowed him to be tested. He was severely tested twice. In the first test, Satan was allowed to take all Job had but not to touch his person. In one day, Job's entire world crumbled. Messengers brought catastrophic news. The first messenger delivered the news that the Sabeans had killed his servants tending the oxen and donkeys, and carried the animals away (Job 1:15). There are a few mentions of Sabeans in scripture. They may have been descendants of Cush, "And the sons of Cush; Seba, and Havilah, and Sabtah, and Raamah, and Sabtecha: and the sons of Raamah; Sheba, and Dedan" (Genesis 10:7). The Greek historian, Herodotus described them as men of great stature, and that is similar to Isaiah's description.

> Thus saith the LORD, The labour of Egypt, and merchandise of Ethiopia and of the Sabeans, men of stature, shall come over unto thee, and they shall be thine: they shall come after thee; in chains they shall come over, and they shall fall down unto thee, they shall make supplication unto thee, saying, Surely God is in thee; and there is none else, there is no God. (Isaiah 45:14).

While the first messenger was still speaking, another messenger came and told Job that fire had "fallen from heaven" and burned up his flock and the servants that were with them (Job 1:16). While the second messenger was speaking, a third messenger came and told him the Chaldeans had taken away the camels and killed the servants that were watching them (Job 1:17). Some theologians believe the Chaldeans were descendants of Chesed, the nephew of Abraham, and brother of Rebekah.

And it came to pass after these things, that it was told Abraham, saying, Behold, Milcah, she hath also born children unto thy brother Nahor; Huz his firstborn, and Buz his brother, and Kemuel the father of Aram, And Chesed, and Hazo, and Pildash, and Jidlaph, and Bethuel. And Bethuel begat Rebekah: these eight Milcah did bear to Nahor, Abraham's brother. (Genesis 22:20-23)

They may also derive their name from the land of Ur of the Chaldees, the land Abraham's father was from. "And Haran died before his father Terah in the land of his nativity, in Ur of the Chaldees" (Genesis 11:28). The Chaldeans are described as a warlike people.

Behold ye among the heathen, and regard, and wonder marvellously: for I will work a work in your days, which ye will not believe, though it be told you. For, lo, I raise up the Chaldeans, that bitter and hasty nation, which shall march through the breadth of the land, to possess the dwellingplaces that are not theirs. They are terrible and dreadful: their judgment and their dignity shall proceed of themselves. Their horses also are swifter than the leopards, and are more fierce than the evening wolves: and their horsemen shall spread themselves, and their horsemen shall come from far; they shall fly as the eagle that hasteth to eat. (Habakkuk 1:5-8)

While the third messenger spoke, a fourth messenger delivered the harshest blow of all. While Job's sons and daughters were celebrating in the eldest brother's house, a "great wind from the wilderness" struck the house's four corners, causing it to fall upon them, and they were dead (Job 1:18-19). The loss of Job's financial assets was nothing compared to the loss of servants he had probably employed for many years, but the loss of all his beloved children was unimaginable.

What does one do when everything he has is suddenly gone, and all of one's children are snatched away at the same time? It is more than most people can bear. Most people would cry out, why? Haven't I been faithful? Haven't I served the Lord well? What have I done that this trouble should fall on me? Why am I in the midst of a storm? One could well have compassion upon them if they did wonder why. But Job responded in a manner of one whose faith in God had not wavered.

> Then Job arose, and rent his mantle, and shaved his head, and fell down upon the ground, and worshipped, And said, Naked came I out of my mother's womb, and naked shall I return thither: the LORD gave, and the LORD hath taken away; blessed be the name of the LORD. In all this Job sinned not, nor charged God foolishly. (Job 1:20-22)

Amid chaos and trials, Job worshipped, and he blessed the name of the Lord. Oh, for the faith, perseverance, and steadfast obedience of Job!

Job's test did not end there. God held him up to Satan as one whom he had allowed Satan to destroy all he owned without a cause, yet he had held onto his integrity and remained upright (Job 2:3). But Satan reminded God that he had protected Job's person from being touched.

> And Satan answered the LORD, and said, Skin for skin, yea, all that a man hath will he give for his life. But put forth thine hand now, and touch his bone and his flesh, and he will curse thee to thy face. And the LORD said unto Satan, Behold, he is in thine hand; but save his life. So went Satan forth from the presence of the LORD, and smote Job with sore boils from the sole of his foot unto his crown. And he took him a potsherd to scrape himself withal; and he sat down among the ashes. (Job 2:4-8)

Job was afflicted with an indescribable skin illness. A once great man now sat in the ashes scraping himself with a piece of broken pottery. Yet he did not turn against God, even when his wife challenged his faith.

> Then said his wife unto him, Dost thou still retain thine integrity? curse God, and die. But he said unto her, Thou speakest as one of the foolish women speaketh. What? shall we receive good at the hand of God, and shall we not receive evil? In all this did not Job sin with his lips. (Job 2:9-10))

Job maintained his integrity against all odds. His patience while enduring severe tests of faith stands today as a paragon of virtue for anyone suffering. Three friends visit Job.

> Now when Job's three friends heard of all this evil that was come upon him, they came every one from his own place; Eliphaz the Temanite, and Bildad the Shuhite, and Zophar the Naamathite: for they had made an

appointment together to come to mourn with him and to comfort him. (Job 2:11)

Job's friends come to mourn with him and comfort him. His condition had caused such a physical change that they did not recognize him. They wept, tore their mantles, and sprinkled dust upon their heads towards heaven, symbolizing their devastation at seeing Job so sick. The friends commiserated with Job in silence for seven days. Sometimes, it is enough for a friend just to be there. The presence of a caring individual speaks volumes.

After this opened Job his mouth, and cursed his day. And Job spake, and said, Let the day perish wherein I was born, and the night in which it was said, There is a man child conceived. (Job 3:1-3)

Job spoke first. He did not curse God but bemoaned the day he was born. It would have been better never to have lived at all or died at birth than to have lived to suffer as he is. Then Job's friends gave a series of speeches to which he responded. Much of their speeches attempted to explain why God allows people to suffer (Chapters 4-25). Job's friends meant well, but the overall idea was that Job suffered because he had done something wrong. They encouraged him to admit his wrong and repent, and God would bless him again. Sometimes, if you cannot say something good, just say nothing at all. Job called them "miserable comforters" and said if he were in their place, he would speak words that "assuaged" their grief.

Then Job answered and said, I have heard many such things: miserable comforters are ye all. Shall vain words have an end? or what emboldeneth thee that thou answerest? I also could speak as ye do: if your soul were in my soul's stead, I could heap up words against you, and shake mine head at you. But I would strengthen you with my mouth, and the moving of my lips should asswage your grief. (Job 16:1-5)

Another friend Elihu, who was younger than the other men, arrived after the first three friends but was there during their speeches. Being the youngest there, he waited until they and Job had finished their speeches before he made the longest speech of all.

Then was kindled the wrath of Elihu the son of Barachel the Buzite, of the kindred of Ram: against Job was his wrath kindled, because he justified himself rather than God. Also against his three friends was his wrath kindled, because they had found no answer, and yet had condemned Job. (Job 32:2-3)

He condemned Job for declaring his innocence, condemned his friends for discontinuing their speeches, and declared the greatness of God. His speech was followed by God dramatically appearing and speaking from a whirlwind, fulfilling Job's desire to speak with him face to face. Job and his friends had spoken of high and lofty subjects in their speeches, the stars, animals, the working of nature, and the universe. As wise men of the East, they had most likely studied the stars and were familiar with the constellations and their courses. Their calendar was a lunar calendar based on the moon's orbit. But God reminded Job that he laid the earth's foundations, put the stars into orbit, and made the constellations.

> Canst thou bind the sweet influences of Pleiades, or loose the bands of Orion? Canst thou bring forth Mazzaroth in his season? or canst thou guide Arcturus with his sons? Knowest thou the ordinances of heaven? canst thou set the dominion thereof in the earth? Canst thou lift up thy voice to the clouds, that abundance of waters may cover thee? Canst thou send lightnings, that they may go, and say unto thee, Here we are? (Job 38:31-35)

Job had studied these constellations and had an exceptional understanding of the cosmos, but he could not answer God's questions about them or understand the ordinances of heaven (Laws of the Universe). His knowledge was limited to what he could observe, but the Creator, the Almighty God of heaven and earth, had placed the universe into being and done so however he pleased. Job had to admit he had no answer.

> Behold, I am vile; what shall I answer thee? I will lay mine hand upon my mouth. Once have I spoken; but I will not answer: yea, twice; but I will proceed no further. (Job 40:4-5)

Further, Job humbled himself under the hand of Almighty God and repented. "I have heard of thee by the hearing of the ear: but now mine eye seeth thee. Wherefore I abhor myself, and repent in dust and ashes" (Job 42:5-6).

God turned Job's situation around. He gave him "beauty for ashes, the oil of joy for mourning, the garment of praise for the spirit of heaviness" (Isaiah 61:3). God condemned Job's friends for speaking against Job and commanded them to bring a burnt offering to Job and have him pray for them. After Job prayed for them, God accepted their offering.

> And it was so, that after the LORD had spoken these words unto Job, the LORD said to Eliphaz the Temanite, My wrath is kindled against thee, and against thy two friends: for ye have not spoken of me the thing that is right, as my servant Job hath. Therefore take unto you now seven bullocks and seven rams, and go to my servant Job, and offer up for yourselves a burnt offering; and my servant Job shall pray for you: for him will I accept: lest I deal with you after your folly, in that ye have not spoken of me the thing which is right, like my servant Job. So Eliphaz the Temanite and Bildad the Shuhite and Zophar the Naamathite went, and did according as the LORD commanded them: the LORD also accepted Job. (Job 42:7-9)

Job prayed for his friends, and the Lord restored all he had lost (Job 42:10).

Job's friends and family came and ate with him and mourned with him. Each brought him money and a golden earring. God blessed Job to have double the wealth he had before his testing, and to father seven more sons and three more daughters.

> So the LORD blessed the latter end of Job more than his beginning: for he had fourteen thousand sheep, and six thousand camels, and a thousand yoke of oxen, and a thousand she asses. He had also seven sons and three daughters. (Job 42:12-13)

As a father, Job did an unusual thing. His daughters were the fairest in the land (Job 42:14). Usually, the eldest son received a double inheritance and cared for his sisters and mother if she remained. Job gave his daughters an inheritance with their brothers (Job 42:15). The Bible says Job lived another 140 years and saw four generations of his descendants.

The Septuagint, an ancient Greek translation of the Hebrew Old Testament, says he lived another 170 years.

And Job lived after affliction a hundred and seventy years: and all the years he lived were two hundred and forty: and Job saw his sons and his sons' sons, the fourth generation (Job 42:16 LXX).

The Septuagint also claims Job was the grandson of Esau and a ruler of Edom. Jobab ben Zerah (Yōbāb ben-Zerah) was a king of ancient Edom, according to Genesis Chapter 36. He succeeded Bela ben Beor in the kingship of the Edomites. He ruled from Bozrah. Husham succeeded him.

And Job died, an old man and full of days: and it is written that he will rise again with those whom the Lord raises up. This man is described in the Syriac book living in the land of Ausis, on the borders of Idumea and Arabia: and **his name before was Jobab; and having taken an Arabian wife, he begot a son whose name was Ennon. And he himself was the son of his father Zare, one of the sons of Esau**, and of his mother Bosorrha, so that he was the fifth from Abraam. And these were the kings who reigned in Edom, which country he also ruled over: first, Balac, the son of Beor, and the name of his city was Dennaba: but after Balac, Jobab, who is called Job, and after him Asom, who was governor out of the country of Thaeman: and after him Adad, the son of Barad, who destroyed Madiam in the plain of Moab; and the name of his city was Gethaim. And friends who came to him were Eliphaz, of the children of Esau, king of the Thaemanites, Baldad sovereign the Sauchaeans, Sophar king of the Minaeans. (Job 42:17 LXX)

Though we may not know for sure who Job was, we know God praised him as a man blameless and a father who loved his children and brought them up to worship the one true God, and that is the faith all men should have. In all that he did, Job demonstrated the epitome of a force to be reckoned with, a formidable man.

19 DANIEL

In the third year of the reign of Jehoiakim king of Judah came Nebuchadnezzar king of Babylon unto Jerusalem, and besieged it. (Daniel 1:1)

Daniel was from one of the noble families of Judah. Judah had been made a tributary to Egypt, and Jehoiakim was placed on the throne as a vassal king. The Pharaoh of Egypt invaded Babylon. Nebuchadnezzar, king of Babylon, defeated the Egyptians at the Battle of Charchemish. Being allied with Egypt, Jerusalem was also invaded and subdued by Nebuchadnezzar. This happened in 606 or 605 B.C. This was the first Babylonian invasion. There would be two other invasions, one around 597 B.C. and the final siege in 586 B.C. when the city would be torched and Solomon's Temple destroyed. Most survivors of this final siege would be taken captive and relocated to Babylon. God allowed Judah to be taken because of her disobedience.

And the Lord gave Jehoiakim king of Judah into his hand, with part of the vessels of the house of God:

which he carried into the land of Shinar to the house of his god; and he brought the vessels into the treasure house of his god. And the king spake unto Ashpenaz the master of his eunuchs, that he should bring certain of the children of Israel, and of the king's seed, and of the princes; Children in whom was no blemish, but well favoured, and skilful in all wisdom, and cunning in knowledge, and understanding science, and such as had ability in them to stand in the king's palace, and whom they might teach the learning and the tongue of the Chaldeans. (Daniel 1:2-4)

Nebuchadnezzar took some of the vessels out of the Temple and placed them in the house of his god. More temple vessels would be taken during the next two invasions but would be restored under the reign of the Persian King, Cyrus. Nebuchadnezzar took the best and brightest children of noble birth with him to train for leadership positions in his administration. These were the elite of the elite, the best-looking and the most skilled. Daniel and his friends Hananiah, Mishael, and Azariah were among these children.

And the king appointed them a daily provision of the king's meat, and of the wine which he drank: so nourishing them three years, that at the end thereof they might stand before the king. Now among these were of the children of Judah, Daniel, Hananiah, Mishael, and Azariah. (Daniel 1:5-6)

The children were given the same food and wine served to the king. They would undergo a three-year education period before entering civil service. Ashpenaz, the chief of the officials, assigned the Hebrew children new names. Daniel, which means "God is my judge," had his name changed to Belteshazzar. His new name may mean "Bel protects my life" according to the Brown-Driver-Briggs Lexicon. Daniel never uses the name when referring to himself in scripture.

Hananiah, whose name means "Yah has favored," was given the name Shadrach, meaning "royal" or "the great scribe." Mishael, whose name means "who is what God is," was given the name Meshach, meaning "guest of a king." Azariah, whose name means "Yah has helped or protected," was given the name Abednego, meaning "servant of Nebo." All four youths were from the royal bloodline.

> But Daniel purposed in his heart that he would not defile himself with the portion of the king's meat, nor with the wine which he drank: therefore he requested of the prince of the eunuchs that he might not defile himself. (Daniel 1:8)

The king's diet was very different from the Kosher diet the Hebrew children were used to eating. In addition, the food may have been offered to idols. Their tables had the best wines and the most extravagant bread, meats, fruits, and other delicacies. Daniel was determined not to eat the unclean food. God had given Daniel great favor with the official over them, and Daniel asked to be excused from the king's table. Ashpenaz was concerned that Daniel's health would suffer as a consequence. It would put his life in jeopardy should he appear to be ill.

Then said Daniel to Melzar, whom the prince of the eunuchs had set over Daniel, Hananiah, Mishael, and Azariah, Prove thy servants, I beseech thee, ten days; and let them give us pulse to eat, and water to drink. Then let our countenances be looked upon before thee, and the countenance of the children that eat of the portion of the king's meat: and as thou seest, deal with thy servants. So he consented to them in this matter, and proved them ten days. (Daniel 1:11-14)

Daniel was not discouraged by the refusal of Ashpenaz to allow him to be excused from eating the king's food. His faith would not allow him to compromise his principles. His focus was on obeying the precepts of God set forth in the Mosaic laws.

There comes a time in all of our lives when we must choose whom we will serve, whether the gods of this world or the Creator of the Universe. Daniel chose the Lord.

Ashpenaz had set Melzar over Daniel and his three friends. Daniel immediately took his request to Melzar, telling him to test his words by giving him and his friends vegetables to eat and water to drink. If their appearance suffered compared to the children eating the king's food, he could do what he had to do.

God touched the heart of Melzar with compassion and favor for Daniel, and he let Daniel and his friends eat a vegetarian diet for ten days. At the end of the ten days, Daniel and his friends appeared better and fatter than those who ate the king's food.

> As for these four children, God gave them knowledge and skill in all learning and wisdom: and Daniel had understanding in all visions and dreams. (Daniel 1:17)

Daniel and his friends were given divine knowledge and understanding of all the Babylonian literature and studies in higher mathematics, science, languages, and ancient writings. This knowledge was beyond the gifts they were born with and had gained great skills in. They were endowed with immeasurable natural wisdom, knowledge, and understanding in "all learning and wisdom" above what they were taught during the three years. Daniel was gifted with the amazing ability to interpret all visions and dreams. At the end of the three years, Ashpenaz presented Daniel and his friends before Nebuchadnezzar.

> And the king communed with them; and among them all was found none like Daniel, Hananiah, Mishael, and Azariah: therefore stood they before the king. And in all matters of wisdom and understanding, that the king enquired of them, he found them ten times better than all the magicians and astrologers that were in all his realm. (Daniel 1:19-20)

Nebuchadnezzar tested the overall knowledge of the children he had brought from Jerusalem to identify the most promising young people. He found Daniel and his friends to be ten times better than his own magicians and astrologers. Daniel, and his friends had refused to be conformed to the lifestyle and religion of Babylon. They had been kept by the power of God and exalted above their brethren and the wise men of Babylon. Nebuchadnezzar placed them into service in his royal court.

"And Daniel continued even unto the first year of King Cyrus" (Daniel 1:21). Daniel served as a high government official in the king's court through Nebuchadnezzar's reign (606 B.C.-539 B.C.) and the reign of four other kings, including that of Cyrus of Persia who defeated Babylon and freed Israel.

Nebuchadnezzar's First Dream (Daniel 2)

And in the second year of the reign of Nebuchadnezzar Nebuchadnezzar dreamed dreams, wherewith his spirit was troubled, and his sleep brake from him. (Daniel 2:1)

King Nebuchadnezzar had a dream. When he awoke, he could not remember the dream, only that it was very disturbing. He could not sleep because of the dream.

The king called for his magicians, astrologers, sorcerers, and the Chaldean wise men to tell him what the dream was and give him the interpretation. Babylon's chief wise men prided themselves on their wisdom and knowledge of sciences, languages, and interpretation of dreams. The Chaldeans respectfully asked the king to tell them the dream, and they would give him the interpretation.

> The king answered and said to the Chaldeans, The thing is gone from me: if ye will not make known unto me the dream, with the interpretation thereof, ye shall be cut in pieces, and your houses shall be made a dunghill. But if ye shew the dream, and the interpretation thereof, ye shall receive of me gifts and rewards and great honour:

therefore shew me the dream, and the interpretation thereof. (Daniel 2:5-6)

Nebuchadnezzar could not remember what he had dreamed, only that he was much troubled in spirit because of it. He demanded they tell him the dream and give them the interpretation or be cut in pieces while still alive and their houses demolished. If they told him the dream and gave him the interpretation, they would receive many gifts and rewards and have great honors heaped upon them.

The wise men asked again that he tell them the dream. They were stumped. They needed time. It was impossible to interpret the dream without knowing what it was. Nebuchadnezzar knew they were stalling for time. He knew their interpretation would be false even if he could recall the dream and tell them.

The Chaldeans told him that no man would be able to tell him the dream, "There is not a man upon the earth that can shew the king's matter: therefore there is no king, lord, nor ruler, that asked such things at any magician, or astrologer, or Chaldean" (Daniel 2:10). It was inconceivable that the king would ask of them such a thing.

For this cause the king was angry and very furious, and commanded to destroy all the wise men of Babylon. And the decree went forth that the wise men should be slain; and they sought Daniel and his fellows to be slain. (Daniel 2:12-13)

Nebuchadnezzar became furious and decreed that all

the wise men be slain. As Daniel and his friends had shown themselves to be among the wisest, it was also a death sentence for them.

> Then Daniel answered with counsel and wisdom to Arioch the captain of the king's guard, which was gone forth to slay the wise men of Babylon: He answered and said to Arioch the king's captain, Why is the decree so hasty from the king? Then Arioch made the thing known to Daniel. (Daniel 2:14-15)

Daniel did not panic. He respectfully approached Arioch, the captain of the king's guard, and asked why the king had decreed such a thing so hurriedly. Arioch explained to Daniel that the king had a dream to which no one could tell or show him the interpretation. Daniel went to his house and shared the trouble with Hananiah, Mishael, and Azariah. He asked them to pray that God would reveal the dream so they would not perish with the rest of the wise men of Babylon.

The dream and the interpretation was revealed to Daniel "in a night vision." "Then Daniel blessed the God of heaven" (Daniel 2:19). The dream was revealed to Daniel, and he went to Arioch, who brought him before the king.

Daniel first informed the king that men could not make the interpretation, but God is the revealer of secrets. The dream Nebuchadnezzar had was of things that would come to pass. Nebuchadnezzar had seen a colossal and very bright image in his dream. The head was fine gold, the breast, and arms were silver, the belly and thighs were brass, the legs were iron, and the feet were part iron and part clay (Daniel 2:32-33). As Nebuchadnezzar stared in amazement at the image, a stone cut without hands struck it on its feet and broke it into tiny dust-like pieces. The wind carried the pieces away, and the stone that crushed them became a great mountain that filled the earth (Daniel 12:35).

The dream interpretation was that God had given Nebuchadnezzar a kingdom, power, strength, and glory (Daniel 2:36-37). He had given him a vast dominion and made him ruler over all. Nebuchadnezzar was the head of gold (Babylon). Nebuchadnezzar's kingdom would be crushed, and another kingdom would arise that was inferior to him. The Persian kingdom arose under Cyrus and crushed the Babylonian kingdom.

A third kingdom would arise, crush the second kingdom and rule the earth. The Macedonian empire arose under Alexander the Great and his successors and crushed the Persian empire. The feet and toes of the image were part clay and part iron. The third kingdom would be divided, but part of it would dominate over the other. It would be partly strong and partly broken. There would be marriages and affinities among the kingdoms to strengthen their alliance, but it would not unite them, as iron does not mix with clay. Alexander's kingdom was divided between his four generals. Two of those kingdoms dominated the others. Marriages and alliances between the kingdoms did not strengthen their alliance and did not unite them.

In the days of this last kingdom, God would set up a kingdom that would break the other kingdoms into pieces and consume them. All the other kingdoms had been transitory. They came, and they passed, but this kingdom would stand forever. It would be a universal kingdom, an unchangeable kingdom, an immutable kingdom, an eternal kingdom – the Kingdom of Christ.

"The great God hath made known to the king what shall come to pass hereafter: and the dream is certain, and the interpretation thereof sure" (Daniel 2:45). God had made known to Nebuchadnezzar future events. Daniel told the dream exactly; Nebuchadnezzar knew his interpretation was true.

Nebuchadnezzar fell on his face and confessed that Daniel's God was Lord of all, the revealer of secrets. He gave Daniel many gifts and made him ruler over all of Babylon and chief over all the wise men. But Daniel remembered his prayer partners. "Then Daniel requested of the king, and he set Shadrach, Meshach, and Abednego, over the affairs of the province of Babylon: but Daniel sat in the gate of the king" (Daniel 2:49). When God brings you into your destiny, don't forget to thank those he has used in your life as support, inspiration and prayer partners.

Nebuchadnezzar's Second Dream (Daniel 4)

"I Nebuchadnezzar was at rest in mine house, and flourishing in my palace" (Daniel 4:4). King Nebuchadnezzar was experiencing a time of peace and prosperity, having subdued all serious threats to his kingdom. He was content in the palace when he had another dream that terrified him.

He commanded all the wise men of Babylon to interpret the dream, but as usual, they could not. Lastly, Daniel came before the king, whom he called Belteshazzar.

O Belteshazzar, master of the magicians, because I know that the spirit of the holy gods is in thee, and no secret troubleth thee, tell me the visions of my dream that I have seen, and the interpretation thereof. (Daniel 4:9)

When Daniel heard the dream, he was troubled. He had to deliver a hard message to Nebuchadnezzar. The dream only boded well for the enemies of the king. Nebuchadnezzar had seen a very tall tree in the middle of the earth that grew and was strong. The tree's height reached the sky and was visible to all the earth (Daniel 4:11). The tree was beautiful. It produced such an abundance of fruit that it fed every creature on the earth. Its shade protected the beasts of the fields, and its branches were home to the birds.

As Nebuchadnezzar stared at the tree, a holy emissary from heaven came down and ordered the tree be hewed down, its branches cut off, the leaves be shaken off, the fruit be scattered, the beasts to get away from it, and the birds to leave from its branches. Nevertheless, the tree was not to be destroyed completely. The stump and roots were to be left in the earth, protected by a band of iron in a field of tender grass.

The description changes from that of a tree to a man. The man was to live outdoors with the beasts in the field, where he would be exposed to the elements of nature

(Daniel 4:15). His heart was to be changed from a man's heart to a beast's heart until seven times had passed over him. The man would believe he was an animal until the time of his penalty passed.

The watcher proclaimed the decree was one from the watchers and commanded: "by the word of the holy ones to the intent that the living might know that the most high ruleth in the kingdom of men, and giveth it to whomsoever he will, and setteth up over it the basest of men" (4:17).

Nebuchadnezzar asked Daniel to make known the interpretation of the dream. He saw that Daniel was troubled and told him not to be afraid of telling the dream interpretation (Daniel 4:18).

Daniel said the dream was to them that hated Nebuchadnezzar, and the interpretation benefitted his enemies. The great tree he saw represented him and the vastness of his kingdom. He had prospered. He had protected and fed the people of the earth under his dominion.

The decree that Nebuchadnezzar be hewed down, yet not destroyed, was the judgment of the Most High upon the king. He would lose his mind and, because of his strange behavior, be driven from the palace to live with the beasts in the field; he would eat grass and be exposed to nature's elements until the time of the decree passed so that he might know the sovereign God rules in heaven and earth and that he gives "to whomsoever he will" (Daniel 4:25). He would continue to live as a beast of the field until he repented and acknowledged that God was sovereign.

Nevertheless, the stump or root of his kingdom would remain and be restored once he repented. Finally, Daniel urged the king to repent and show mercy to the poor; perhaps the peace he now experienced would be lengthened.

Daniel's interpretation was sure, and all the events foretold in Nebuchadnezzar's dream came to pass. Nebuchadnezzar was walking pridefully in one of the sumptuous palaces he had built in Babylon at the end of twelve months, congratulating himself on having built this magnificent empire "by the might of my power, and for the honour of my majesty" (Daniel 4:28-30).

"Pride goeth before destruction, and an haughty spirit before a fall" (Proverbs 16:18). Before Nebuchadnezzar could finish his pompous presumptions, a voice spoke from heaven, saying, "O king Nebuchadnezzar, to thee it is spoken; The kingdom is departed from thee" (Daniel 4:31). He heard the voice say what the watcher in his dream told him. He would be driven to live with the beast of the field for seven years until he repented and gave glory to the Most High God.

In the very same hour, the prophecy was fulfilled. Nebuchadnezzar was deprived of his mental faculties, and he was driven from men to live with the beast of the field. His hair grew out until it looked like the feathers of an eagle, and his nails grew so long that they were like a bird's claws.

And at the end of the days I Nebuchadnezzar lifted up mine eyes unto heaven, and mine understanding returned unto me, and I blessed the most High, and I praised and honoured him that liveth for ever, whose dominion is an everlasting dominion, and his kingdom is from generation to generation. (Daniel 4:34)

At the end of the seven years, the king raised his eyes toward heaven. This act of submission and surrender caused God to restore his understanding. He acknowledged the Most High God and blessed his holy name.

As a result of his repentance, Nebuchadnezzar's kingdom was restored to him, and he gave praise and glory to the only wise God.

The Handwriting On The Wall (Daniel 5)

Belshazzar was the grandson of King Nebuchadnezzar. He called Nebuchadnezzar his "father," but the word used is a generic term and can mean a father, grandfather, or ancestor (Daniel 5:13).

Belshazzar made a great feast for a thousand of his nobles, concubines and wives. While they were having a good time drinking wine, he commanded that the golden and silver vessels his grandfather had taken out of the Temple in Jerusalem be brought, and they drank from them.

Nebuchadnezzar had been humbled by an encounter with the God of Daniel, but now his grandson profaned the vessels from the House of the Lord "and praised the gods of gold, and of silver, of brass, of iron, of wood, and of stone" (Daniel 5:4).

> In the same hour came forth fingers of a man's hand, and wrote over against the candlestick upon the plaister of the wall of the king's palace: and the king saw the part of the hand that wrote. (Daniel 5:5)

One must be careful to respect the things of God. In the very hour that Belshazzar and his guests were using vessels set aside for sacred service, God showed that wrath was poured upon him. He saw a man's hand write on the wall of the palace. He suddenly sobered from his drunken state. He became weak in his body, and his knees knocked against one another as he trembled with fear.

The king called for all the wise men of his kingdom and offered them rewards of the highest caliber if they could read the handwriting on the wall and give him the interpretation, but none could. The queen came into the banquet and told him not to worry. There was one in the kingdom that could read the writing and give him the interpretation.

> Forasmuch as an excellent spirit, and knowledge, and understanding, interpreting of dreams, and shewing of hard sentences, and dissolving of doubts, were found in the same Daniel, whom the king named Belteshazzar: now let Daniel be called, and he will shew the interpretation. (Daniel 5:12)

Daniel was called before the king. He recalled to Belshazzar how his grandfather had been humbled when he lifted his heart up in his pride. He had been made to live as a beast in the field for seven years until he knew that the Most High God ruled in the heavens.

Though Belshazzar knew what happened to his grandfather, he did not humble his heart but drank from the vessels brought out of the House of the Lord and praised idol gods. He did not glorify God.

Then was the part of the hand sent from him; and this writing was written. And this is the writing that was written, MENE, MENE, TEKEL, UPHARSIN. This is the interpretation of the thing: MENE; God hath numbered thy kingdom, and finished it. TEKEL; Thou art weighed in the balances, and art found wanting. PERES; Thy kingdom is divided, and given to the Medes and Persians. (Daniel 5:24-28)

Daniel gave the interpretation of the dream. His kingdom was finished. He had been weighed in the balances and found wanting. The kingdom would be taken from him and given to the Medes and Persians. Belshazzar had Daniel decorated with a scarlet robe and a gold chain around his neck and issued a proclamation that made him the third ruler in the land. But it did not change the judgment against him.

"In that night was Belshazzar, the king of the Chaldeans, slain. And Darius the Median took the kingdom, being about threescore and two years old" (Daniel 5:30-31). That very night, Belshazzar was assassinated, and the kingdom was taken from him and given to the Medes and Persians.

Daniel In The Lion's Den (Daniel 6)

It pleased Darius to set over the kingdom an hundred and twenty princes, which should be over the whole kingdom; And over these three presidents; of whom Daniel was first: that the princes might give accounts unto them, and the king should have no damage. (Daniel 6:1-2)

King Darius, the Median, overthrew the Babylonian government. He appointed 120 princes over the kingdom. He appointed three regional administrators over the princes, of whom Daniel was first.

Then this Daniel was preferred above the presidents and princes, because an excellent spirit was in him; and the king thought to set him over the whole realm. (Daniel 6:3)

Daniel found favor in the eyes of the king because of his excellent spirit. The king thought to set him over his entire kingdom. Whenever God promotes you, others will seek to destroy you. The other regional administrators and princes sought to find a fault in Daniel; any small infraction could be used against him.

But such was Daniel's integrity, such was his excellence, such was the spirit of God in him, that his character and life were spotless. They could find no fault in his life or work, so they thought to persecute him because of his faith.

Taking advantage of the king's ego, they proposed he issue a decree that made him divinity for thirty days.

Anyone found asking a petition of any other god would suffer the death penalty. This flattered the king's vanity, and he did so.

> Now when Daniel knew that the writing was signed, he went into his house; and his windows being open in his chamber toward Jerusalem, he kneeled upon his knees three times a day, and prayed, and gave thanks before his God, as he did aforetime. (Daniel 6:10)

Hearing the decree had been signed, Daniel boldly and purposefully went to his house, opened the windows where he could be seen praying toward Jerusalem, and prayed three times a day, as he had always done. Daniel had not sought this conflict but did not avoid it when it was thrust upon him. Daniel's enemies were watching his every move. They hurried back to the king when they saw him praying to the Lord God of Israel. They informed the king that Daniel was praying to God contrary to his decree. The penalty was that he be thrown into the lion's den.

> Then the king, when he heard these words, was sore displeased with himself, and set his heart on Daniel to deliver him: and he laboured till the going down of the sun to deliver him. (Daniel 6:14)

The King loved Daniel and tried to think of a way around his decree, but the signed decree of a king could not be reversed.

Sadly, King Darius had the decree enforced. Daniel was cast into the lion's den. The king fasted and walked the floor all night long. He was unable to sleep. Early in the morning, he ran to the lion's den and called for Daniel.

> Then said Daniel unto the king, O king, live for ever. My God hath sent his angel, and hath shut the lions' mouths, that they have not hurt me: forasmuch as before him innocency was found in me; and also before thee, O king, have I done no hurt. (Daniel 6:21-22)

The angel of the Lord had shut the mouths of the lions, and Daniel emerged from the den without even a hair out of place. He stood for his faith, and that great faith kept him safe even in the midst of lions.

The men who had accused Daniel were thrown into the lion's den with their families and broken into pieces by the lions before they even came to the bottom of the den. When you contrive to dig a ditch for the children of God, know that you are digging a ditch for yourself. God protects those who serve him. The King wrote another decree that the God of Daniel was the only God.

> I make a decree, That in every dominion of my kingdom men tremble and fear before the God of Daniel: for he is the living God, and stedfast for ever, and his kingdom that which shall not be destroyed, and his dominion shall be even unto the end. He delivereth and rescueth, and he worketh signs and wonders in heaven and in earth, who hath delivered Daniel from the power of the lions. (Daniel 6:26-27)

So Daniel prospered under Darius, as he had prospered under the kings before him. Daniel had visions of end times during his time in captivity that are of such an important nature and so integral to the history of mankind that we cannot expound on them in this work. All that he did, he did with an excellent spirit. He was truly a force to be reckoned with, a formidable man.

20 THE THREE HEBREW BOYS

Nebuchadnezzar the king made an image of gold, whose height was threescore cubits, and the breadth thereof six cubits: he set it up in the plain of Dura, in the province of Babylon. (Daniel 3:1)

Shadrach, Meshach and Abednego are examples of men who chose to stand with the Lord, even when they had to stand all alone. King Nebuchadnezzar caused a massive image of gold to be made. The height was sixty cubits (about ninety feet). It was six cubits wide (about nine feet). This occurred after his first dream but before the humbling experience of his second dream.

He may have conceived the idea from Daniel's interpretation of his first dream, where a head of gold symbolized his kingdom in the image of his dream.

> Thou, O king, art a king of kings: for the God of heaven hath given thee a kingdom, power, and strength, and glory. And wheresoever the children of men dwell, the beasts of the field and the fowls of the heaven hath he

given into thine hand, and hath made thee ruler over them all. Thou art this head of gold. (Daniel 2:37-38)

Nebuchadnezzar summoned all the officials of the Babylonian empire to the dedication ceremony.

Then the princes, the governors, and captains, the judges, the treasurers, the counsellors, the sheriffs, and all the rulers of the provinces, were gathered together unto the dedication of the image that Nebuchadnezzar the king had set up; and they stood before the image that Nebuchadnezzar had set up. (Daniel 3:3)

The brightness of the colossal golden image shining in the sun must have been a fearsome sight. The announcement was made that when the people heard "the sound of the cornet, flute, harp, sackbut, psaltery, dulcimer, and all kinds of musick," they were to "fall down and worship the golden image" (Daniel 3:5). Anyone who did not obey would be cast alive into a blazing furnace.

The music played, summoning the people to fall down and worship the golden image. Shadrach, Meshach, and Abednego, the three Hebrew boys who were friends of Daniel, did not fall down. Daniel may have been away from the empire on the king's business because he was not among the leaders gathered. The Chaldean wise men saw what happened.

Daniel and his friends had refused to eat at the King's table, and God rewarded them with divine intelligence beyond and above the Chaldean mystics and magicians.

Though their lives had been spared due to Daniel interpreting the King's dream, they may have remained jealous of their abilities and the favor shown toward them by Nebuchadnezzar by setting them over the affairs of the province of Babylon.

The Chaldeans went to the King and turned in the Hebrew boys. Shadrach, Meshach, and Abednego were brought up on charges of insubordination to the King, who flew into a royal rage. Shadrach, Meshach, and Abednego had been set into positions of honor and power, princes of the provinces of Babylon by recommendation of Daniel. Now, they found themselves in a life and death situation and in displeasure with the same king who had shown them much favor. Nebuchadnezzar gave them an ultimatum. They were to fall down and worship the golden image when they heard the music. If they did not worship the image, they would be cast into the furnace, "and who is that God that shall deliver you out of my hands?" (Daniel 3:15b.)

> Shadrach, Meshach, and Abednego, answered and said to the king, O Nebuchadnezzar, we are not careful to answer thee in this matter. If it be so, our God whom we serve is able to deliver us from the burning fiery furnace, and he will deliver us out of thine hand, O king. But if not, be it known unto thee, O king, that we will not serve thy gods, nor worship the golden image which thou hast set up. (Daniel 3:16-18)

Shadrach, Meshach, and Abednego did not equivocate; they did not excuse themselves. They stood firm. They stood bold. They answered that the God they served could deliver them from the fiery furnace, and he would deliver them out of the hand of the king. But if he did not deliver them, they would not serve his gods or worship the golden image.

The expression on Nebuchadnezzar's face showed he was filled with fury at the disobedience of these young men. He ordered the furnace to be heated seven times hotter than it already was. He commanded the mightiest men in his army to tie up the Hebrew boys and throw them into the furnace. They were bound fully clothed and cast into the furnace. The flames from the fire killed the men that threw them in the furnace.

Then Nebuchadnezzar the king was astonied, and rose up in haste, and spake, and said unto his counsellors, Did not we cast three men bound into the midst of the fire? They answered and said unto the king, True, O king. He answered and said, Lo, I see four men loose, walking in the midst of the fire, and they have no hurt; and the form of the fourth is like the Son of God. (Daniel 3:24-25)

Nebuchadnezzar couldn't believe his eyes. The three Hebrew boys had been thrown into the furnace and should have perished immediately like the soldiers that tossed them in, but as he looked, he saw them walking around in the furnace alive and well, and a fourth person was with them that he thought looked like "the Son of God."

The King called for the three Hebrew boys to come forth. All the people with him saw that not even a hair on their heads had been singed. They were in perfect condition. They did not even smell of smoke.

> Then Nebuchadnezzar spake, and said, Blessed be the God of Shadrach, Meshach, and Abednego, who hath sent his angel, and delivered his servants that trusted in him, and have changed the king's word, and yielded their bodies, that they might not serve nor worship any god, except their own God. Therefore I make a decree, That every people, nation, and language, which speak any thing amiss against the God of Shadrach, Meshach, and Abednego, shall be cut in pieces, and their houses shall be made a dunghill: because there is no other God that can deliver after this sort. (Daniel 3:28-29)

Shadrach, Meshach, and Abednego had chosen death rather than sin against God and were miraculously preserved in the fire by his mighty power. Nebuchadnezzar blessed the God of Shadrach, Meshach, and Abednego and ordered that anyone who spoke irreverently of him be killed and their houses demolished. The glorious deliverance, by which God brought them forth, changed the heart of the king, and he acknowledged the one true God and "promoted Shadrach, Meshach, and Abednego, in the province of Babylon" (Daniel 3:30).

When all the world opposes you, know that you and the God you serve are more than the world against you. Stand fast in your faith; he will deliver you in all circumstances. Like the three Hebrew boys, you will be a force to be reckoned with, formidable men.

21 ZACHARIAS

There was in the days of Herod, the king of Judaea, a certain priest named Zacharias, of the course of Abia: and his wife was of the daughters of Aaron, and her name was Elisabeth. And they were both righteous before God, walking in all the commandments and ordinances of the Lord blameless. (Luke 1:5-6)

Zacharias was a priest ministering in the Temple in the days of "Herod, the king of Judaea." The name, Zacharias, is the same as Zechariah in the Old Testament and means "Yahweh Remembers." When the descendants of Aaron, the first high priest, grew so numerous that all could not officiate together at the Tabernacle, King David divided them into twenty-four classes or courses so that they ministered by turns, each family serving a whole week (1 Chronicles Chapters 23 through 24). Zachariah was of the course or lot of Abia (Hebrew - "Abijah"), the eighth course.

Zacharias was married to Elisabeth. Her name is the same as Elisheba (oath of God), the name of Aaron's wife

(Exodus 6:23). Being of the house of Aaron, she was the daughter of a priest; thus, she and Zacharias were descended from the family of Amram, the father of Moses, Aaron, and Miriam, three of the most powerful leaders in Jewish history.

Moses was the first Great Deliverer of Israel and the writer of the entire Pentateuch or Torah (the first five books of the Old Testament). There was never such a leader before or after him who spoke with God face to face as one speaks to a friend (Exodus 33:11; Deuteronomy 34:10). Aaron was appointed a spokesperson for Moses. He was the first High Priest of Israel. He and his sons were given the priesthood, and the other Levitical families were given to them to assist them. Miriam was the first woman to be called a prophetess in the Bible. She was the leader of the women of Israel and was highly used of God.

Not only were Zacharias and Elisabeth of impeccable lineage, but the Bible also says they were "righteous before God." They lived in obedience to God, walking in his "commandments and ordinances." No fault was found in their conduct. Impeccable credentials, background, character, and conduct do not guarantee that you will not encounter trials in life. "And they had no child, because that Elisabeth was barren, and they both were now well stricken in years" (Luke 1:7).

In a society where it was considered divine retribution if you did not have children, Zacharias and Elisabeth must have suffered unduly in the perceptions of the community. "Oh, they must have sinned in some way if the Lord withholds children from them."

Zacharias had not taken a second wife to produce descendants as some men would have done, and now they were both up in years. Their childless situation was hopeless. Perhaps they even felt forgotten by God, but God remembers those who serve him. It was impossible that they would produce offspring at their age, but "The things which are impossible with men are possible with God" (Luke 18:27), and one day while Zacharias was going about his priestly duties burning incense upon the altar of incense while the people prayed outside, an angel appeared to him "standing on the right side of the altar of incense" (Luke 1:11).

The angel announced their prayers had been heard, and Elisabeth would conceive and bear a son.

> But the angel said unto him, Fear not, Zacharias: for thy prayer is heard; and thy wife Elisabeth shall bear thee a son, and thou shalt call his name John. And thou shalt have joy and gladness; and many shall rejoice at his birth. For he shall be great in the sight of the Lord, and shall drink neither wine nor strong drink; and he shall be filled with the Holy Ghost, even from his mother's womb. And many of the children of Israel shall he turn to the Lord their God. (Luke 1:13-16)

They were to call their son John, meaning "Yahweh has been gracious" or "Yahweh has shown favor." Their son would be born a Nazirite. The Nazarite vow was a vow of consecration, "a vow of a Nazarite to separate themselves unto the Lord" (Numbers 6:2). The Hebrew noun used as Nazarite is "nazir," and it means "devoted one." The word "separate" in the clause "separate themselves unto the

Lord" is the Hebrew verb "nazar," meaning abstaining from, to dedicate, to consecrate, to be separated from their community for a time.

The requirements of the Nazarite vow are found primarily in the Old Testament passages of Numbers 6:1 - 21, Judges 13:5 - 7, 16:17, and Amos 2:11 - 12. It was generally done by the individual's own choice, but two individuals in the Old Testament and one in the New Testament were under the vow at birth. Samuel was presented to God by his parents, a vow his mother vowed before his conception (1 Samuel 2:8-28). Samson received the Nazarite vow by divine command to his parents before his birth (Judges 13:1-5), and in the New Testament, the son of Zacharias and Elisabeth (Luke 1:13-17).

"And Zacharias said unto the angel, Whereby shall I know this? for I am an old man, and my wife well stricken in years" (Luke 1:18). Zacharias needed a sign, and it was given. He would be speechless until the day of the birth because he doubted (Luke 1:19-20). Sometimes, we have to be stilled to see the salvation of the Lord. The birth and work of this child would be so integral to the baptism and work of Jesus that any doubt would not be tolerated.

The people wondered why Zacharias was taking so long in the temple. When he came out, he could not speak but made signs, and they could tell he had seen a vision. When the days of his service were over, he went home. Elisabeth did indeed conceive a child and did not go out into the public for five months. By that time, her condition would be so evident that the mouths of the accusers would be silenced.

And after those days his wife Elisabeth conceived, and hid herself five months, saying, Thus hath the Lord dealt with me in the days wherein he looked on me, to take away my reproach among men. (Luke 1:24-25)

Because they were found faithful, Elisabeth and Zacharias joined a list of parents in the Bible who were childless at the beginning but who were later blessed with children: Abraham and Sarah, Isaac and Rebekah, Jacob and Rachel, Manoah and his wife (the parents of Samson), Hannah and Elkanah (the parents of Samuel), the great woman of Shunem and her husband (2 Kings 4:8-17). Sometimes we have to wait on greatness.

When Mary was visited by the angel Gabriel, she was told that her relative, Elisabeth, had also conceived a child and traveled expeditiously to see her. At her greeting, the baby leaped within Elisabeth's womb because she was pregnant with the Messiah, and Elisabeth was filled with the Holy Spirit.

"Now Elisabeth's full time came that she should be delivered; and she brought forth a son" (Luke 1:57). The child was born, and Elisabeth and Zacharias' neighbors came to rejoice with them. On the eighth day, the child was circumcised in accordance with Hebrew law and given his name. Ordinarily, a son would be named after the father, but Elisabeth said no, "he shall be called John" (Luke 1:60). Those who came to perform the circumcision said none of their kindred had that name. Zacharias could not speak, so they made signs to him asking him what the name of the child was to be. He responded by writing, "His name is John" Luke 1:63).

And his mouth was opened immediately, and his tongue loosed, and he spake, and praised God. And fear came on all that dwelt round about them: and all these sayings were noised abroad throughout all the hill country of Judaea. And all they that heard them laid them up in their hearts, saying, What manner of child shall this be! And the hand of the Lord was with him. (Luke 1:64-66)

Zacharias received his ability to speak again upon his compliance with the angel's command that the child would be named John. Zacharias was filled with the holy ghost and prophesied.

The Song of Zacharias (Luke 1:67-79)

Blessed be the Lord God of Israel; for he hath visited and redeemed his people,

And hath raised up an horn of salvation for us in the house of his servant David;

As he spake by the mouth of his holy prophets, which have been since the world began:

That we should be saved from our enemies, and from the hand of all that hate us;

To perform the mercy promised to our fathers, and to remember his holy covenant;

The oath which he sware to our father Abraham,

That he would grant unto us, that we being delivered out of the hand of our enemies might serve him without fear,

In holiness and righteousness before him, all the days of our life.

And thou, child, shalt be called the prophet of the Highest: for thou shalt go before the face of the Lord to prepare his ways;

To give knowledge of salvation unto his people by the remission of their sins,

Through the tender mercy of our God; whereby the dayspring from on high hath visited us,

To give light to them that sit in darkness and in the shadow of death, to guide our feet into the way of peace.

The Forerunner

"And the child grew, and waxed strong in spirit, and was in the deserts till the day of his shewing unto Israel" (Luke 1:80). He grew in stature and divine illumination. When he was thirty years old, he came into the fulfillment of the prophecy as the forerunner of the Messiah, preaching repentance and turning away from sins in the wilderness. Zacharias waited on the Lord. He was of good courage, and that courage bought him into a destiny he could only have imagined as the father of John the Baptist and made him a force to be reckoned with, a formidable man.

22 JOSEPH OF NAZARETH

Now the birth of Jesus Christ was on this wise: When as his mother Mary was espoused to Joseph, before they came together, she was found with child of the Holy Ghost. (Matthew 1:18)

I hereby nominate Joseph of Nazareth for the earthly Father of All-Time award. Joseph worked as a skilled carpenter, an honorable occupation. His lineage was impeccable. He was a true Hebrew, a descendant of Abraham, and a descendant of King David.

Joseph carefully chose a young lady from among his people to marry. Mary was also a Hebrew, a descendant of Abraham, and a descendant of King David.

As customary in the Hebrew culture, Joseph married Mary but waited for a year to consummate the union. During this time, he worked continually to prepare a house for them to live in. Mary, of course, was living with her parents. Hebrew women prepared for their groom an entire year before they came together.

Joseph was suddenly made aware that the girl he married but had never touched was pregnant. According to the law, he had every right to divorce her and make her a public example for others. But Joseph, a man of faith, did not want to embarrass Mary and considered quietly putting her away without broadcasting it to the community. He knew what people would say and how they would treat Mary if they found out. She would be an outcast.

Thank God Joseph did not act rashly. He took his time contemplating the situation. His is a lesson we can all take to heart. When faced with a difficult decision, wait on the Lord. Meditate until He comes to the rescue. While Joseph was giving the matter thought, he had an epiphany.

But while he thought on these things, behold, the angel of the Lord appeared unto him in a dream, saying, Joseph, thou son of David, fear not to take unto thee Mary thy wife: for that which is conceived in her is of the Holy Ghost. And she shall bring forth a son, and thou shalt call his name JESUS: for he shall save his people from their sins. Now all this was done, that it might be fulfilled which was spoken of the Lord by the prophet, saying, Behold, a virgin shall be with child, and shall bring forth a son, and they shall call his name Emmanuel, which being interpreted is, God with us. (Matthew 1:20-23)

Joseph has given us great hope and an excellent example. We see from his case that God may answer us in a dream. He may have someone call and give us guidance. He may send someone to us with a word of wisdom. There are endless ways that God may choose to answer us if we wait patiently. But by all means, we must not act in haste.

> Then Joseph being raised from sleep did as the angel of the Lord had bidden him, and took unto him his wife: And knew her not till she had brought forth her firstborn son: and he called his name JESUS. (Matthew 1:24-25)

Because Joseph was a man of faith, he believed and was obedient. He took Mary for his wife and "knew her not" until the child was born. By faith, he became the earthly father of the greatest descendant of his people, the savior of the world, The Messiah, the Bright and Morning Star, the Lion of the Tribe of Judah, the Root of David, the blessed and only potentate, the Lord of Lords, and King of Kings. That made Joseph a force to be reckoned with, a formidable man.

23 SIMEON

And, behold, there was a man in Jerusalem, whose name was Simeon; and the same man was just and devout, waiting for the consolation of Israel: and the Holy Ghost was upon him. (Luke 2:25)

Simeon was among the many Israelites waiting for the consolation of Israel, The Messiah.

And when the days of her purification according to the law of Moses were accomplished, they brought him to Jerusalem, to present him to the Lord; (As it is written in the law of the Lord, Every male that openeth the womb shall be called holy to the Lord;) And to offer a sacrifice according to that which is said in the law of the Lord, A pair of turtledoves, or two young pigeons. (Luke 2:22-24)

Mary and Joseph coming to the temple accomplished two purposes: it fulfilled the Mosaic law concerning bringing an offering after a woman's purification from giving birth (Leviticus 12:6-8), and it fulfilled the Mosaic law concerning the dedication of firstborn males to the Lord (Exodus 13:2, 12).

Mary fulfilled the seven days of separation for ceremonial uncleanness required for the mother of a newborn male child. She and Joseph obeyed the law first by having the child circumcised when He was eight days old. This was the sign and seal of the covenant God made with Abraham (Genesis 17), which was required of every Jewish male. Even though Christ was God manifested in the flesh and did not require circumcision, he "suffered it to be so" so that he might "fulfill all righteousness" (Matthew 3:15).

These rites of the Mosaic Law—circumcision and purification— were intended as ceremonial rituals that foreshadowed the purification by the blood of Christ for the imperfections of man and the sin inherited by every child of man. In the cases of Mary and her Child, these rites were not necessary. Still, Mary submitted herself and her child to the ceremonial requirements and was willingly obedient to that Divine Law under which she was born and had lived.

When the Christ Child was circumcised, Mary and Joseph gave Him the name Jesus in obedience to the angel's proclamation. (Matthew 1:21). Jesus is the Greek word translation for the Hebrew word "Yeshua," "YAHshua," or "Yehoshua," meaning "Savior" or "Salvation."

But circumcision was only the beginning. When the child was forty days old, Mary and Joseph had to come to the temple for the purification rites for women described in Leviticus 12. They also had to "redeem" the child since he was Mary's firstborn (Exodus 13:1–12).

The firstborn males belonged to the Lord and were dedicated to the service of the tabernacle. God spared the firstborn when he passed over Egypt, executing the firstborn males of every house because of the sign of the blood on their doors. Afterward, God appointed the Levites to serve in the tabernacle in their stead. Even though the Levites were taken as substitutes for every firstborn male, the firstborn males were brought to be presented to the Lord and redeemed.

According to the Law of Moses, they brought a humble sacrifice of two turtledoves or two young pigeons to God for the purification offering. This offering was permitted for those who were too poor to afford a lamb as the offering (see Leviticus 12:8). Their humble sacrifice would suggest they were too poor to bring a lamb (2 Corinthians 8:9). But they brought in their arms the Lamb slain from the foundation of the world (Revelation 13:8), he who when he offered himself once and for all purged the sins of those who believe.

> How much more shall the blood of Christ, who through the eternal Spirit offered himself without spot to God, purge your conscience from dead works to serve the living God? And for this cause he is the mediator of the new testament, that by means of death, for the redemption of the transgressions that were under the first testament, they which are called might receive the promise of eternal inheritance. (Hebrews 9:14-15)

> But this man, after he had offered one sacrifice for sins for ever, sat down on the right hand of God; From henceforth expecting till his enemies be made his footstool. For by one offering he hath perfected for ever them that are sanctified. (Hebrews 10:12-14)

There was a remnant of believing Jews in Jerusalem who waited with great anticipation for their Redeemer. Among these devoted Israelites was Simeon. It had been revealed to him that he would not die until he had seen the Salvation of God (Luke 2:26). If you have been waiting on God to do something in your life, and it appears that it's taking a long time, hold on. You will see the Salvation of the Lord.

Simeon was led by the Spirit to the temple on the very day that Mary and Joseph came with the Christ Child. Simeon took the Christ Child in his arms and spoke words that are as powerful today as they were then.

> Then took he him up in his arms, and blessed God, and said, Lord, now lettest thou thy servant depart in peace, according to thy word: For mine eyes have seen thy salvation, Which thou hast prepared before the face of all people; A light to lighten the Gentiles, and the glory of thy people Israel. (Luke 2:28-32)

His parents wondered at the words spoken. Simeon blessed God; he gave all praises to God that he had been privileged to have seen the Messiah with his own eyes. After so many years of waiting, Simeon saw the Messiah. He declared Jesus to be "A light to lighten the Gentiles, and the glory of thy people Israel."

Simeon's Song (Luke 2:34-35)

And Simeon blessed them, and said unto Mary his mother, Behold, this child is set for the fall and rising again of many in Israel; and for a sign which shall be spoken against; (Yea, a sword shall pierce through thy own soul also,) that the thoughts of many hearts may be revealed. (Luke 2:34-35)

Simeon praised God and blessed Mary and Joseph, but he did not bless the Baby because Jesus is the source of every blessing. He prophesied that Jesus was appointed and set by God for the fall of the reprobate and the rise of those who believed he was the Christ.

Simeon referenced the piercing of his flesh and that Mary's own soul would also be pierced with a sword. Mary did feel "the sword" in her heart repeatedly as she watched her Son during His ministry and then stood at the cross where He was crucified (John 19:25–27).

Having obeyed the Law in everything, Mary and Joseph returned to Nazareth, which would be our Lord's home until He started His official ministry. Luke reports that the lad developed physically, mentally, socially, and spiritually. "And the Child grew, and waxed strong in spirit, filled with wisdom and the grace of God was upon him" (Luke 2:39-40).

By faith, Simeon saw the Messiah. He was a force to be reckoned with, a formidable man.

24 JOHN THE BAPTIST

Behold, I will send my messenger, and he shall prepare the way before me: and the Lord, whom ye seek, shall suddenly come to his temple, even the messenger of the covenant, whom ye delight in: behold, he shall come, saith the LORD of hosts. (Malachi 3:1)

John the Baptist, the forerunner of Christ, was a miracle child. His mother, Elisabeth, was a relative of Mary, the mother of Jesus. His father, Zacharias, was a priest. Elisabeth was barren, and they were of age when an angel appeared to Zacharias and announced his wife would birth a son, and they were to call him "John."

He was set aside for greatness from conception. He was to be a Nazarite, one separated to the work of the Lord.

Elisabeth and Zacharias were of the house of Aaron. Thus, she and Zacharias were descended from the family of Amram, the father of Moses, Aaron, and Miriam, three of the most powerful leaders in Jewish history. Moses, the first and great deliverer of Israel, wrote the first five books of the Bible. Aaron and his sons were given the priesthood, and the other Levitical families were given to assist them. Miriam was the first woman to be called a prophetess in the Bible and was highly used of God.

Elisabeth, and the mother of Jesus, were related. Elisabeth conceived six months before Mary's immaculate conception.

John's age when he entered his public ministry is based on the age of Jesus, since they were only months apart. Jesus was about thirty years of age when he entered ministry. "Jesus himself began to be about thirty years of age" (Luke 3:23a). Thirty years is considered the age of full maturity for Hebrew males. In the Torah (first five chapters of the Hebrew Bible, Tanach), the Levites (priests) only began to work in the Tabernacle at thirty (see Numbers 4:47). "From thirty years old and upward even unto fifty years old, every one that came to do the service of the ministry, and the service of the burden in the tabernacle of the congregation" (Numbers 4:47). At fifty, they were exempted from physical labor, though still expected to attend in the temple (Numbers 8:26).

The Mishnah is a written interpretation of oral Jewish traditions documented by Jewish scholars (Rabbis). It tells us that thirty was considered the height of strength for a Jewish male.

> He [Rabbi Shmuel HaKatan] used to say: At five years of age the study of Scripture; At ten the study of Mishnah; At thirteen subject to the commandments; At fifteen the study of Talmud; At eighteen the bridal

canopy; At twenty for pursuit [of livelihood]; **At thirty the peak of strength**; At forty wisdom; At fifty able to give counsel; At sixty old age; At seventy fullness of years; At eighty the age of "strength"; At ninety a bent body; At one hundred, as good as dead and gone completely out of the world. (Avoth Chapter 5 Mishnah 21)

Three events are recorded as occurring at the beginning of the ministry of Jesus: His baptism by John the Baptist, His temptation in the wilderness, and His first miracle of turning water into wine at the wedding in Cana.

John the Baptist was the prophesied forerunner of Jesus. He went before our Lord preaching repentance, baptizing, and announcing that the Messiah was come. "The voice of him that crieth in the wilderness, Prepare ye the way of the LORD, make straight in the desert a highway for our God" (Isaiah 40:3).

> In those days came John the Baptist, preaching in the wilderness of Judaea, And saying, Repent ye: for the kingdom of heaven is at hand. For this is he that was spoken of by the prophet Esaias, saying, The voice of one crying in the wilderness, Prepare ye the way of the Lord, make his paths straight. (Matthew 3:1-3)

John the Baptist made it clear that he was not the Christ, only the announcer that he was come. He baptized with water, but the Messiah would baptize with the Spirit.

> I indeed baptize you with water unto repentance: but he that cometh after me is mightier than I, whose shoes I

am not worthy to bear: he shall baptize you with the Holy Ghost, and with fire: Whose fan is in his hand, and he will throughly purge his floor, and gather his wheat into the garner; but he will burn up the chaff with unquenchable fire. (Matthew 3:11-12)

John saw Jesus coming to the river where he was baptizing and recognized him as the one that was prophesied to come. "The next day John seeth Jesus coming unto him, and saith, Behold the Lamb of God, which taketh away the sin of the world" (John 1:29). John recognized that he had need of being baptized by Jesus and not Jesus being baptized of him. But Jesus humbled himself and submitted to baptism as he would submit to death on the cross.

But John forbad him, saying, I have need to be baptized of thee, and comest thou to me? And Jesus answering said unto him, Suffer it to be so now: for thus it becometh us to fulfil all righteousness. Then he suffered him. And Jesus, when he was baptized, went up straightway out of the water: and, lo, the heavens were opened unto him, and he saw the Spirit of God descending like a dove, and lighting upon him: And lo a voice from heaven, saying, This is my beloved Son, in whom I am well pleased. (Matthew 3:14-17)

The seal of the Father was seen by the Spirit in the form of a dove descending upon him and a voice from heaven declaring that God was pleased.

But Herod the tetrarch, being reproved by him for Herodias, his brother Philip's wife, and for all the evils which Herod had done, Added yet this above all, that he shut up John in prison. (Luke 3:19-20)

John was bold enough to stand before Herod and deliver the message that he had sinned by taking his brother's ex-wife and brought all the other evils he had committed before him. Herod had him thrown into prison. Know that when you stand on the authority of the Word of God, that authority will be challenged by the adversary. His wife, Herodias, demanded the execution of John, but Herod feared John because he knew he was a holy man. He also feared the people because they counted John as a prophet.

Therefore Herodias had a quarrel against him, and would have killed him; but she could not: For Herod feared John, knowing that he was a just man and an holy, and observed him; and when he heard him, he did many things, and heard him gladly. (Mark 6:19-20)

But Herodias waited for a timely opportunity when she could put her scheme into action. Herod had a grand birthday celebration. The daughter of Herodias danced for Herod, and he was so pleased that he promised to give her anything she wanted. Her mother had instructed her beforehand to ask for the head of John the Baptist on a platter (Matthew 14:8).

And the king was sorry: nevertheless for the oath's sake, and them which sat with him at meat, he commanded it to be given her. And he sent, and beheaded John in the prison. And his head was brought in a charger, and given to the damsel: and she brought it to her mother.

And his disciples came, and took up the body, and buried it, and went and told Jesus. (Matthew 14:9-12)

Herodias reminds one of Jezebel when she killed the prophets of the Lord. There will be times when you may be persecuted for righteousness' sake. John extolled all that was holy, and all that was right in his preaching. As a result, he was martyred, but he had this testimony of our Lord. "For I say unto you, Among those that are born of women there is not a greater prophet than John the Baptist: but he that is least in the kingdom of God is greater than he" (Luke 7:28). He was a force to be reckoned with, a formidable man.

25 THE APOSTLES

Now the names of the twelve apostles are these; The first, Simon, who is called Peter, and Andrew his brother; James the son of Zebedee, and John his brother; Philip, and Bartholomew; Thomas, and Matthew the publican; James the son of Alphaeus, and Lebbaeus, whose surname was Thaddaeus; Simon the Canaanite, and Judas Iscariot, who also betrayed him. (Matthew 10:2-4)

Apostle (Greek – "Apostolos") simply means "a messenger," "a delegate," or "one sent forth with orders." It is most commonly applied to the original twelve apostles chosen by Christ and the one chosen to take the place of Judas Iscariot. The writer of Hebrews used it in reference to Jesus Christ.

> Wherefore, holy brethren, partakers of the heavenly calling, consider the Apostle and High Priest of our profession, Christ Jesus. (Hebrews 3:1)

Jesus had many disciples. He taught them for three years before choosing twelve as his inner circle and sending them forth. He would later send seventy others to go before him, witnessing every place he was to go.

> After these things the Lord appointed other seventy also, and sent them two and two before his face into every city and place, whither he himself would come. Therefore said he unto them, The harvest truly is great, but the labourers are few: pray ye therefore the Lord of the harvest, that he would send forth labourers into his harvest. (Luke 10:1-2)

Jesus endowed them with power against unclean spirits, power to raise the dead, and power to heal all sickness and disease. The first twelve were specifically sent to the lost sheep of the house of Israel (Matthew 10:5-7).

> Again the next day after John stood, and two of his disciples; And looking upon Jesus as he walked, he saith, Behold the Lamb of God! And the two disciples heard him speak, and they followed Jesus. (John 1:35-37)

Andrew and Peter were two brothers. Andrew and another disciple of John the Baptist were present when John called Jesus "the Lamb of God" and followed him. Jesus turned and asked why they were following him. They went with him and spent the day listening to him.

> One of the two who heard John speak, and followed him, was Andrew, Simon Peter's brother. He first findeth his own brother Simon, and saith unto him, We have found the Messias, which is, being interpreted, the Christ. And he brought him to Jesus. And when Jesus beheld him, he said, Thou art Simon the son of Jona:

thou shalt be called Cephas, which is by interpretation, A stone. (John 1:40-42)

Simon and Andrew were fishermen. Jesus later saw the brothers fishing as he walked by the sea of Galilee.

And he saith unto them, Follow me, and I will make you fishers of men. And they straightway left their nets, and followed him. (Matthew 4:19-20)

At his command, the brothers left their nets and became disciples, confirming their roles in the church's history. Peter swore he would never deny Jesus, but while he hung on the cross, he became afraid, along with the other disciples, and denied knowing the Savior. Tradition states that Peter was crucified by Nero about 64 A.D. It is said that he was crucified upside down because he did not consider himself worthy to die in the same manner as Jesus. According to tradition, Andrew was crucified around 60 A.D.

James and John, the sons of Zebedee, were fishermen. They worked on their father's ship. Going forward from Andrew and Peter, Jesus saw James and John with their father, Zebedee, in their ship and told them to follow him. They did not hesitate but left their nets and followed the master to their destinies. John was called the "beloved disciple." He was the only one to die a natural death.

Most conservative scholars have concluded that John wrote the Gospel of John, 1 John, II John, III John, and the book of Revelation. Together they are known as the Johannine writings. John stood near the cross when Jesus was crucified along with some of the women. The other disciples fled.

Jesus surnamed James and John "the sons of thunder," probably because of their zeal for preaching the gospel. "And James the son of Zebedee, and John the brother of James; and he surnamed them Boanerges, which is, The sons of thunder" (Mark 3:17).

James is the only death recorded in the Bible of the original apostles, except for the suicide of Judas. "Now about that time Herod the king stretched forth his hands to vex certain of the church. And he killed James the brother of John with the sword" (Acts 12:1-2).

Matthew states that the mother of James and John came and requested of Jesus that her sons sit on either side of him in his kingdom, but Mark 10 states it was the sons of thunder who asked it of Jesus themselves.

Then came to him the mother of Zebedee's children with her sons, worshipping him, and desiring a certain thing of him. And he said unto her, What wilt thou? She saith unto him, Grant that these my two sons may sit, the one on thy right hand, and the other on the left, in thy kingdom. But Jesus answered and said, Ye know not what ye ask. Are ye able to drink of the cup that I shall drink of, and to be baptized with the baptism that I am baptized with? They say unto him, We are able. And he saith unto them, Ye shall drink indeed of my cup, and be baptized with the baptism that I am baptized with: but to sit on my right hand, and on my left, is not mine to give, but it shall be given to them for whom it is prepared of my Father. (Matthew 20:20-23)

Jesus said that honor was not his to give but would be given to those for whom the Father prepared it.

Philip and Nathanael were friends. The next day after Andrew and Peter found Jesus, he found Philip.

The day following, Jesus would go forth into Galilee, and findeth Philip, and saith unto him, Follow me. Now Philip was of Bethsaida, the city of Andrew and Peter. Philip findeth Nathanael, and saith unto him, We have found him, of whom Moses in the law, and the prophets, did write, Jesus of Nazareth, the son of Joseph. (John 1:43-45)

Jesus found Philip and told him to follow after him. Philip then found his friend, Nathanael (also called Bartholomew), and told him the good news that they had found the Messiah. Both followed Jesus and assumed their places as disciples.

It was Nathanael who asked, "Can anything good come out of Nazareth?" (John 1:46.) Philip told him to come and see for himself. Seeing Nathanael coming to him, Jesus said, "Behold an Israelite indeed, in whom is no guile!" (John 1:47.)

How Philip died is uncertain, but tradition says he was martyred around 80 A.D. It is unclear when or how Nathanael was martyred. They were doing the work of spreading the Gospel. History has not recorded all of it.

Matthew was a tax collector, one hated by most Jews.

And as Jesus passed forth from thence, he saw a man, named Matthew, sitting at the receipt of custom: and he saith unto him, Follow me. And he arose, and followed him. (Matthew 9:9)

When Jesus told Matthew to follow him, he arose without hesitation and became a disciple, going from a hated position to one of glory. Matthew wrote the Gospel of Matthew. It is unclear where and how Matthew suffered martyrdom.

Thomas is also called Didymus (John 11:16). The phrase "doubting Thomas" derives from Thomas not believing the disciples had seen the risen Savior. When he had seen and touched the risen Savior for himself, then he believed.

Jesus saith unto him, Thomas, because thou hast seen me, thou hast believed: blessed are they that have not seen, and yet have believed. (John 20:29)

Tradition states Thomas was martyred about 72 A.D. by being stabbed with a spear.

James, the son of Alphaeus, is only mentioned three times in the Bible. It is unclear when and how this apostle was martyred. He is sometimes confused with James the Just, the brother of our Lord. Though our history of these disciples and the apostles is incomplete, their work in the kingdom is well documented in the Book of Life. Their reward is sure.

Lebbaeus, whose surname was Thaddaeus, was also called Jude or Judas Thaddeus. How and where Judas Thaddeus suffered martyrdom is unclear.

Simon the Canaanite is also called Zelotes (Luke 6:15). How and where Simon was martyred is unclear.

Judas Iscariot, the traitor, was the treasurer. He betrayed our Lord for thirty pieces of silver. Judas tried to repent and return the money, but it was not accepted. He committed suicide. "And he cast down the pieces of silver in the temple, and departed, and went and hanged himself" (Matthew 27:5). What a sad epitaph.

Matthias was chosen in the place of Judas.

> Wherefore of these men which have companied with us all the time that the Lord Jesus went in and out among us, Beginning from the baptism of John, unto that same day that he was taken up from us, must one be ordained to be a witness with us of his resurrection. (Acts 1:21-22)

The disciples chose from among themselves a replacement for the apostleship of Judas. The criteria was that the person had been a disciple of Christ for the three years he had taught them and had been a witness to the resurrected Savior.

Two disciples were nominated to replace Judas Iscariot: Joseph, called Barsabas; and Matthias. The disciples asked God for guidance and chose Matthias by casting lots. It was an accepted method for making choices in that time.

And they appointed two, Joseph called Barsabas, who was surnamed Justus, and Matthias. And they prayed, and said, Thou, Lord, which knowest the hearts of all men, shew whether of these two thou hast chosen, That he may take part of this ministry and apostleship, from which Judas by transgression fell, that he might go to his own place. And they gave forth their lots; and the lot fell upon Matthias; and he was numbered with the eleven apostles. (Acts 1:23-26)

Little is known of this apostle, and it is unclear how and when he suffered martyrdom.

Paul was accepted by the disciples as an apostle because of his personal encounter with the Savior on the road to Damascus. The writer of most of the New Testament is discussed in a separate chapter.

The apostles, and their fellow disciples, were highly used of God. The birth of the church on Pentecost, a Jewish feast day, was the beginning of the transition from Judaism to Gentile Christianity. In accordance with the command of Jesus, one hundred twenty of His disciples and followers gathered in the upper room for prayer. The Holy Spirit came upon them with visible and audible signs, fulfilling prophecy and proving the resurrection of Christ (Acts 2:1-4). The believers were fused into one unit. They received boldness to speak the Gospel and brave the perils of persecution they would soon face.

The apostolic preaching was a narrative of the life and work of Christ with a defense of his resurrection, followed by a call to repentance in his name. The addresses were saturated with Old Testament quotations and prophecies. The methods of early preaching and current preaching may differ, but the burden of preaching remains the same: The necessity of belief in the risen Christ, repentance both personal and national, and the receiving of the Holy Spirit (Acts 2:8). In addition, where it is accompanied by instruction, one can see an increase in believers as well as their being bound together in common knowledge and common action.

The early church leaders were the apostles; however, the government was essentially democratic. When complaints arose from the Hellenistic Jews that their widows were being neglected in the daily food distribution, the apostles suggested that qualified men be appointed to oversee this part of the church's activities. The "multitude" chose seven men to fulfill this duty.

> And the saying pleased the whole multitude: and they chose Stephen, a man full of faith and of the Holy Ghost, and Philip, and Prochorus, and Nicanor, and Timon, and Parmenas, and Nicolas a proselyte of Antioch: Whom they set before the apostles: and when they had prayed, they laid their hands on them. And the word of God increased; and the number of the disciples multiplied in Jerusalem greatly; and a great company of the priests were obedient to the faith. (Acts 6:5-7)

The leaders of this period were Peter, John, and Stephen. Peter dominated the scene from the opening address on the day of Pentecost. He defended the Christian believers when he and John were accused before the Sanhedrin (Acts 4:5-8).

They were persecuted, they were executed, they suffered hunger and other indescribable hardships because they witnessed Christ. They turned the world upside down (Acts 17:6). Their end is glorious. The walls of the heavenly Jerusalem has twelve foundations with the names of the apostles inscribed upon them. "And the wall of the city had twelve foundations, and in them the names of the twelve apostles of the Lamb" (Revelation 21:14). They were a force to be reckoned with, formidable men.

26 NICODEMUS

There was a man of the Pharisees, named Nicodemus, a ruler of the Jews. (John 3:1)

Nicodemus. His name means "victorious among his people." Nicodemus was no ordinary Jew. He was a Pharisee, the strictest sect of the Jews. They taught and adhered to Judaism's religious, ethical, and ceremonial laws. They believed the only way to God was for a man to keep the law. If a man could be saved through the law or works, they would surely have been accounted righteous. This sect produced some great men: Hillel, the famous doctor of Jewish law; Gamaliel, grandson of Hillel, who had such a high place accorded to him that he was first to have the title of Rabban, higher even than Rabbi or Master, bestowed upon him; his great student Paul called by God to be an Apostle; and Josephus, the most important contemporary Jewish historian of his day.

Nicodemus was an important official. He was a ruler of the Jews. As such, he was a member of the grand Sanhedrin, the judicial and administrative council of the

Jews. Its members were the most powerful, prestigious, and influential men of their day. Their authority was extensive. They were judges, much like the members of the Supreme Court. As a "master of Israel" (John 3:10), he stood out from the standouts as a scribe, a doctor of law, an interpreter of the law, an instructor in the law, and an Old Testament scholar of the highest caliber.

Despite all that he was and all he had, something was missing in his life. But he heard about Jesus, and although many of the Sanhedrin had a vendetta against Jesus, he felt his teachings and miracles were of God.

The same came to Jesus by night, and said unto him, Rabbi, we know that thou art a teacher come from God: for no man can do these miracles that thou doest, except God be with him. (John 3:2)

Tradition tells us that Nicodemus was one of the three richest men in Jerusalem. Though he was preeminent, wealthy, educated, and influential, Nicodemus was drawn to Jesus and sought him out at night.

We are not told why he came at night, but most Bible scholars have given two theories. Some scholars have theorized that as a representative of the Sanhedrin, it would be an offense to his colleagues and incur the wrath of hostile Jews. Other scholars theorize that he would have been very busy during the day, especially since it was Passover time.

With millions of Jews in Jerusalem for the Holy Days, the religious leaders were very busy. Christ had been busy himself. He had purged the temple, throwing everyone out of the marketplace, performed miracles, answered questions concerning His authority, and taught. Both Christ and Nicodemus had been busy during the day, so coming at night would have been the best time for an uninterrupted conversation. Whatever his reason may have been, the point is that he came to Jesus seeking something, and that is the beginning.

His approach to Jesus seems to be sincere. He addresses him respectfully, calling him "Rabbi" (teacher or master), a term of high regard. He says, "we know that Thou art a teacher come from God." The term "we" indicates that at least some of the religious leaders recognized the divine authority by which Jesus spoke. They may not have known who He was, but they knew He was from God and, being religious leaders, wanted to know all about Him. They saw that the miracles He performed could only be done by someone that God was with.

> Jesus answered and said unto him, Verily, verily, I say unto thee, Except a man be born again, he cannot see the kingdom of God. (John 3:3)

"A master of Israel" receives an answer from The Master of the Universe to a question he never even asked. In his omniscience, Christ knows the thoughts and hearts of a man. Jesus immediately addresses the utmost issue of Nicodemus' heart by telling him that the only way he will ever see the Kingdom of God is to be born all over again.

All of Nicodemus' life had led to this moment of truth. For years he had been struggling to be a part of the

Kingdom. His years of keeping the law could not justify him, for if you break even one minor law, you have offended the whole law. His ceremonial rituals and sacrifices were not sufficient to save his soul. His wealth could not buy his way into the Kingdom. His power and influence could not win his way into the Kingdom. Despite his superior education and intellect, he would never enjoy or understand the Kingdom of God, in heaven or on earth, unless he was born again.

> Nicodemus saith unto him, How can a man be born when he is old? can he enter the second time into his mother's womb, and be born? (John 3:4)

Jesus' astonishing response to his unspoken inquiry prompts Nicodemus to ask a question that has reverberated in one fashion or another down through the halls of time in the hearts of those who receive the witness of the Kingdom. The essence of the question is, "How can a man be born again?" It is physically impossible to return back to our mother's wombs and be re-born. The rebirth is a great mystery to those who do not yet understand the plan of salvation.

> Jesus answered, Verily, verily, I say unto thee, Except a man be born of water and of the Spirit, he cannot enter into the kingdom of God. That which is born of the flesh is flesh; and that which is born of the Spirit is spirit. (John 3:5-6)

Jesus, the Author and Finisher of our faith, teaches that to enter into the Kingdom of God, you must have two birthdays or be "born again." The Greek word *"anothen"* used for *"again"* means "from above." There are two births: the physical birth and the spiritual birth. The first birth is the physical birth when we are born into the world. It is the birth of the flesh. The second birth is spiritual, being born of the spirit of God, also known as regeneration. The Holy Spirit recreates us at the point of faith when we receive Christ. "Therefore if any man be in Christ, he is a new creature: old things are passed away; behold, all things are become new" (2 Corinthians 5:17). "But as many as received him, to them gave he power to become the sons of God, even to them that believe on his name: Which were born, not of blood, nor of the will of the flesh, nor of the will of man, but of God" (John 1:12-13).

> Nicodemus answered and said unto him, How can these things be? Jesus answered and said unto him, Art thou a master of Israel, and knowest not these things? (John 3:9-10)

With all his great learning, Nicodemus seemed not to understand the simplicity of the Gospel. Jesus went on to give the illustrious legal expert a lesson illuminating the foundation and qualification for entering the kingdom. The entire message of the Gospel is summarized in this great truth: "For God so loved the world, that he gave his only begotten Son, that whosoever believeth in him should not perish, but have everlasting life" (John 3:16).

Later, when the Jews were murmuring about Jesus. Some believed, and others did not and sought to bring him before the council. Nicodemus said they should not judge the man without hearing him.

Nicodemus saith unto them, (he that came to Jesus by night, being one of them,) Doth our law judge any man, before it hear him, and know what he doeth? They answered and said unto him, Art thou also of Galilee? Search, and look: for out of Galilee ariseth no prophet. And every man went unto his own house. (John 7:50-53)

The Sanhedrin was not favorable toward Nicodemus' urging them to seek Jesus. But finally, Nicodemus showed himself to be a believer when he came together with other secret believers and helped bury the Savior.

And after this Joseph of Arimathaea, being a disciple of Jesus, but secretly for fear of the Jews, besought Pilate that he might take away the body of Jesus: and Pilate gave him leave. He came therefore, and took the body of Jesus. And there came also Nicodemus, which at the first came to Jesus by night, and brought a mixture of myrrh and aloes, about an hundred pound weight. Then took they the body of Jesus, and wound it in linen clothes with the spices, as the manner of the Jews is to bury. Now in the place where he was crucified there was a garden; and in the garden a new sepulchre, wherein was never man yet laid. There laid they Jesus therefore because of the Jews' preparation day; for the sepulchre was nigh at hand. (John 19:38-42)

So, in the end, Nicodemus, a ruler among the Jews, showed that he had come to understand and accept the great principles taught by the Master. That made him a force to be reckoned with, a formidable man.

27 THE NOBLEMAN

So Jesus came again into Cana of Galilee, where he made the water wine. And there was a certain nobleman, whose son was sick at Capernaum. (John 4:46)

The Nobleman was a royal official serving in the court of Herod Antipas. He may have been a relative of the king. The Nobleman had power. He had prestige. He had silver and gold, but his son was sick at Capernaum. His wealth and position could not heal what he held dear to his heart.

> When he heard that Jesus was come out of Judaea into Galilee, he went unto him, and besought him that he would come down, and heal his son: for he was at the point of death. (John 4:47)

The royal officer's son was at the point of death. Capernaum is about a day's journey from Cana, but he made the trip because he heard Jesus had come to Galilee. He was seeking Jesus to ask him to come down to Capernaum and heal his son.

You must seek Jesus with unwavering faith. Jesus said to the nobleman that unless he saw a demonstration of signs and wonders, he would not believe. He had heard of Jesus because his fame had grown. He sought him, hoping for healing for his son, but not knowing he was the Savior. But the nobleman humbled himself. He was desperate. He begged, "Sir, come down ere my child die" (John 4:48). All royal formality was stripped away. He had come this far because he knew Jesus had healed others. Now he believed with his whole heart that Jesus had power over life and death.

It was enough. The master knew when one asked in faith. "Jesus saith unto him, Go thy way; thy son liveth. And the man believed the word that Jesus had spoken unto him, and he went his way" (John 4:50).

The man waited until the next day to take the long journey back home. His servants met him on the way with the news that his son "liveth." He was healed. When the Nobleman enquired when he had begun to heal, they said it was the day before at the seventh hour.

So the father knew that it was at the same hour, in the which Jesus said unto him, Thy son liveth: and himself believed, and his whole house. This is again the second miracle that Jesus did, when he was come out of Judaea into Galilee. (John 4:53-54)

Now the faith of the Nobleman was confirmed. He shared the experience with his entire family, and his whole household was converted. He became a force to be reckoned with, a formidable man.

28 THE ROMAN CENTURION

Now when he had ended all his sayings in the audience of the people, he entered into Capernaum. And a certain centurion's servant, who was dear unto him, was sick and ready to die. (Luke 7:1-2)

Centurions were Roman soldiers, and the Jewish people feared and hated them. Matthew (8:5-13) and Luke (7:1-10) both give us the story of the Roman Centurion who sought Jesus to heal his servant who was very ill.

Luke says the servant was "dear unto him" and "ready to die" (7:2). Matthew says he was grievously sick of the palsy (8:6).

In ancient times, servants sometimes became as close as family members to their masters. Abraham thought he might leave an inheritance to the steward of his house before he had fathered children (Genesis 15:2-3). The entire messianic family stopped to mourn the death of Deborah, who had been Rebekah's nurse (Genesis 35:8).

Matthew says the centurion came to Jesus, begging him to heal his servant (8:5). Luke says the centurion sent the elders of the Jews to beg Jesus to heal his servant (7:3).

And when they came to Jesus, they besought him instantly, saying, That he was worthy for whom he should do this: For he loveth our nation, and he hath built us a synagogue. (Luke 7:4-5)

The Roman Empire ruled Israel at this time. In 63 B.C., the Roman general Pompey the Great captured Jerusalem deposing the ruling Hasmonean dynasty of Judaea, which had been in power since about 140 B.C. The Roman Senate declared Herod the Great "King of the Jews" about 40 B.C. Although Rome recognized Judaism as a legal religion and allowed the Jews to worship freely, they often persecuted the people.

It was highly unusual that a Jew might act on behalf of a Gentile and even more unusual that a man of the centurion's station might ask a Jew to approach someone else, but this was not a typical Roman soldier. The Jewish leaders said he loved the nation of Israel and had built a synagogue for their people. He had done much for Israel and yet did not presume upon his generosities but showed a deep humility. Jesus said, "I will come and heal him" (Matthew 8:7). Luke says the centurion sent friends to tell Jesus not to trouble himself to come to his house.

Then Jesus went with them. And when he was now not far from the house, the centurion sent friends to him, saying unto him, Lord, trouble not thyself: for I am not worthy that thou shouldest enter under my roof:

> Wherefore neither thought I myself worthy to come unto thee: but say in a word, and my servant shall be healed. (Luke 7:6-7)

Matthew also indicates that the centurion did not feel worthy of Jesus entering his house. "The centurion answered and said, Lord, I am not worthy that thou shouldest come under my roof: but speak the word only, and my servant shall be healed" (Matthew 8:8).

The centurion was familiar with the Jewish laws and understood that he was ceremonially unclean to enter the synagogue or the home of a Jew, and it would have made a Jew ceremonially unclean to enter his home. But he also had a great understanding of the authority of Jesus over the universe.

> For I am a man under authority, having soldiers under me: and I say to this man, Go, and he goeth; and to another, Come, and he cometh; and to my servant, Do this, and he doeth it. (Matthew 8:9)

> For I also am a man set under authority, having under me soldiers, and I say unto one, Go, and he goeth; and to another, Come, and he cometh; and to my servant, Do this, and he doeth it. (Luke 7:8)

The centurion understood the principle of authority. One in authority did not have to be present to accomplish a task. Jesus did not have to be in the room to heal his servant because he had authority over nature. Nature was subordinate to him and completely in his power. The centurion was a professional soldier who understood authority because he was a man in authority and a man who was under authority. As a centurion in the Roman army, he commanded 100 men who carried out his orders. He also carried out the orders of his superiors.

A centurion had a proven record in war. They had shown great prowess in defeating the enemy. They had earned the title, and they were paid well. After 15 to 20 years, they were appointed to administrative positions as a senior centurion. The centurion had power; he had authority, but he did not have authority over illness or death. He did not have the power to heal a beloved servant.

One thing this soldier had, though. He had heard about Jesus and had faith that Jesus had the authority to heal. He understood Jesus had the right to exercise that authority, so he came to him as a subordinate.

Jesus was impressed with the centurion's faith. Both Matthew and Luke record that he "marveled" or wondered at such faith.

> When Jesus heard it, he marvelled, and said to them that followed, Verily I say unto you, I have not found so great faith, no, not in Israel. (Matthew 8:10)

The faith of this Gentile was the kind of faith Jesus was looking for among the people chosen by God. This faith was Kingdom faith. God is not a respecter of people. He does not regard ethnicity, race, creed, or color. He looks at the heart, and the heart of the centurion was righteous. The Jews thought they had a free ticket into the Kingdom because they were the children of God. Jesus used the centurion's faith to teach that their religiosity did not guarantee they would enter heaven.

> And I say unto you, That many shall come from the east and west, and shall sit down with Abraham, and Isaac, and Jacob, in the kingdom of heaven. But the children of the kingdom shall be cast out into outer darkness: there shall be weeping and gnashing of teeth. (Matthew 8:11-12)

Those who did not accept Jesus as the Messiah would not enter the Kingdom of God. They would be "cast out into outer darkness" Those who responded to his message and repented would join the faithful Israelites from generations through the ages and have eternal fellowship with God.

> And Jesus said unto the centurion, Go thy way; and as thou hast believed, so be it done unto thee. And his servant was healed in the selfsame hour. (Matthew 8:13)

The centurion's servant was healed the very moment Jesus pronounced the healing based on the centurion's faith. Perhaps you have something or someone in your life that needs healing today. Believe that Jesus is a healer; as you have believed, so be it done unto you. As a centurion, this man had proved himself in battles against the enemies of Rome time after time. As a believer, he would prove himself in the army of the Lord. Now he was a force to be reckoned with, a formidable man.

29 JAIRUS

And, behold, there came a man named Jairus, and he was a ruler of the synagogue: and he fell down at Jesus' feet, and besought him that he would come into his house.
(Luke 8:41)

Jairus ("whom God enlightens") was a ruler of the synagogue. Jesus had just crossed the sea from the country of the Gadarenes, where he had healed a man possessed of demons.

Arriving in Capernaum, Jesus was greeted by crowds who wanted to see his miracles and find healing for themselves or their family and friends. "And it came to pass, that, when Jesus was returned, the people gladly received him: for they were all waiting for him" (Luke 8:40). Sometimes you have to wait on the Savior to see his salvation.

And, behold, there came a man named Jairus, and he was a ruler of the synagogue: and he fell down at

Jesus' feet, and besought him that he would come into his house: (Luke 8:40-42)

The only daughter of Jairus was dying. He had heard about Jesus and came and fell at his feet and begged him to come to his house, "For he had one only daughter, about twelve years of age, and she lay a dying. But as he went the people thronged him" (Luke 8:42). Matthew says he "worshipped him, saying, My daughter is even now dead: but come and lay thy hand upon her, and she shall live" (Matthew 9:18).

Here was one with great authority. He would have been responsible for arranging the synagogue for meetings, receiving the Book of Law from the overseer, appointing who would read the different sections, and maybe leading the council of elders in the synagogue. But his only daughter was lying at the point of death. By this time, he thought she might have already succumbed. And so, he sought out Jesus and fell at his feet, not as a ruler, but in all humility, respect and reverence towards one with higher authority than himself. Mark says, "And besought him greatly, saying, My little daughter lieth at the point of death: I pray thee, come and lay thy hands on her, that she may be healed; and she shall live" (Mark 5:23).

The Master of the Universe stopped what he was doing because this father had faith to believe that he could heal his daughter. "And Jesus arose, and followed him, and so did his disciples" (Matthew 9:19). Amid your trouble, you have only to invite Jesus in, and he will be there.

The crowds thronged in upon the group as they made

their way to Jairus' house. A woman among the crowd had been sick as long as Jairus's daughter had lived. For twelve years, she had suffered from an issue of blood. She knew she would be healed with just one touch of the hem of his garment. Suddenly the hem of his garment was right at her fingertips, and she touched it and felt the healing throughout her body. Jesus knew the touch of faith and stopped an entire entourage on the way to Jairus's house to see who had been healed. Having identified the woman who was healed, Jesus returned his attention to Jairus' daughter.

The woman had been healed, but the time taken to identify her had been costly. One came from Jairus's house with the terrifying confirmation of his worst fears, "Trouble not the master, your daughter is dead."

> While he yet spake, there cometh one from the ruler of the synagogue's house, saying to him, Thy daughter is dead; trouble not the Master. (Luke 8:49)

Jesus had another message for Jairus, "Fear not, believe only, and she shall be made whole" (Luke 8:50). When Jesus is with you, you have nothing to fear. He's coming to your house, and your troubles will be changed, your storms will cease, and everything will be made better. "Yea, though I walk through the valley of the shadow of death, I will fear no evil: for thou art with me; thy rod and thy staff they comfort me" (Psalms 23:4). Believe not the doubters or the skeptics but believe in Jesus.

Jairus believed, and he continued walking with Jesus. When they arrived, the professional mourners had already gathered. With ashes on their heads, they cried and wailed. Jesus said, "Weep not; she is not dead, but sleepeth" (Luke 8:52). The mourners stopped their mourning to laugh with the other scoffers. But Jesus put the naysayers out. Sometimes you have to put the pessimists out of your life and focus only on the Word if you want to see the salvation of the Lord.

> And they laughed him to scorn. But when he had put them all out, he taketh the father and the mother of the damsel, and them that were with him, and entereth in where the damsel was lying. And he took the damsel by the hand, and said unto her, Talitha cumi; which is, being interpreted, Damsel, I say unto thee, arise. And straightway the damsel arose, and walked; for she was of the age of twelve years. And they were astonished with a great astonishment. (Mark 5:40-42)

Jesus turned to the child, took her hand, and said, "Talitha cumi," meaning "Damsel arise." He commanded her to rise, and immediately the child got up and walked. Jesus spoke life into a dead situation then and is still speaking life into dead situations now. Her parents received their child back to life because they had faith.

Jesus told the parents to give the child something to eat. That the child could eat proved she was alive and well, not a spirit returned from the dead. Jairus is an example of a man of faith and a devoted father because when his daughter's condition seemed hopeless, he believed Jesus could turn it around and make her whole again. That makes him a force to be reckoned with, a formidable man.

30 ZACCHAEUS

And Jesus entered and passed through Jericho. And, behold, there was a man named Zacchaeus, which was the chief among the publicans, and he was rich.
(Luke 19:1-2)

Zacchaeus was a chief tax collector. That meant he was an administrator for the Roman government over other tax collectors. They were equivalent to the Internal Revenue Service of our time. Jewish tax collectors were despised by their people. They made themselves wealthy by overcharging the Jewish people and then taking a cut from the taxes gathered. Zacchaeus received a cut from the taxes gathered by other tax collectors whose work he administered.

As head of the customs department at Jericho, Zacchaeus had become a very wealthy man. Jericho was an important center of trade. Its location between points of transport made it a significant custom house. Jericho was where a large quantity of balsam was produced and exported. The balm in the Gilead district came through there before it was shipped to all parts of the world.

> And he sought to see Jesus who he was; and could not for the press, because he was little of stature. And he ran before, and climbed up into a sycamore tree to see him: for he was to pass that way. (Luke 19:3-4)

But on this day, Zacchaeus had something else on his mind. He had obviously heard about Jesus and his teachings. He wanted to see him when he passed through, but being a short man, the crowd was in his way. He unceremoniously climbed a sycamore tree where he would have an unobstructed view. Sometimes, you must get above the crowd to see the Savior clearly.

> And when Jesus came to the place, he looked up, and saw him, and said unto him, Zacchaeus, make haste, and come down; for to day I must abide at thy house. (Luke 19:5)

Jesus, looking up, saw Zacchaeus in the tree and told him to hurry down because he was dining at his house. Jesus did not care what Zacchaeus had done in the past. He did not care that his house was considered unclean by the proper community of Jews. "But he answered and said, I am not sent but unto the lost sheep of the house of Israel" (Matthew 15:24). It was for such as Zacchaeus that Jesus was sent.

"And he made haste, and came down, and received him joyfully" (Luke 19:6). Zacchaeus was astonished that Jesus would come to his house. He was not popular among the people. Zacchaeus was filled with glee. He hurried down and welcomed Jesus to come to his house.

"And when they saw it, they all murmured, saying, That he was gone to be guest with a man that is a sinner" (Luke 19:7). The Jews were upset that Jesus would dine with one whom they considered the chief of sinners and they murmured between themselves. After all, Jericho was one of the cities where priests and Levites lived. Yet Jesus would spend the night with a man the religious leaders hated.

> And Zacchaeus stood, and said unto the Lord; Behold, Lord, the half of my goods I give to the poor; and if I have taken any thing from any man by false accusation, I restore him fourfold. (Luke 19:8)

Zacchaeus showed he truly repented of his sins. He would act to repair what he could by giving half of his wealth to the poor and making restitution to any man he had profited by from bringing him up on false charges.

> And Jesus said unto him, This day is salvation come to this house, forsomuch as he also is a son of Abraham. For the Son of man is come to seek and to save that which was lost. (Luke 19:9-10)

In the very moment that he repented, Zacchaeus was forgiven. He who had been lost was found and restored. He received eternal life. Now, he had a possession that was incorruptible. Now, he was a force to be reckoned with, a formidable man.

31 STEPHEN

And Stephen, full of faith and power, did great wonders and miracles among the people. (Acts 6:8)

Stephen is important in the church's history because he was the first to be martyred for the witness of the Gospel. At the birth of the church on Pentecost, one hundred twenty disciples and followers were gathered in the upper room for prayer. The Holy Spirit came upon them with visible and audible signs, fulfilling prophecy and proving the resurrection of Christ. The believers were fused into one unit. They received boldness to speak the Gospel and brave the perils of persecution they would soon face.

The early church leaders were the apostles, but democratic principles governed them. They had all things in common and lived as a community. The Hellenistic Jews complained that their widows were neglected in the daily distribution of food. The apostles told them to choose qualified men to be appointed to oversee this part of the church's activities.

And the saying pleased the whole multitude: and they chose Stephen, a man full of faith and of the Holy Ghost, and Philip, and Prochorus, and Nicanor, and Timon, and Parmenas, and Nicolas a proselyte of Antioch: Whom they set before the apostles: and when they had prayed, they laid their hands on them. (Acts 6:5-6)

They chose seven men to fulfill this duty. Stephen was one of the seven chosen for relief work. He did not confine his activities to social work, but became an outstanding apologist of the early church and an evangelist. He was full of faith and power of the Holy Ghost and did "great wonders and miracles among the people."

Some false prophets disputed with Stephen but were unsuccessful because he was too full of the Holy Ghost and had been granted divine wisdom. Having been made to look like idiots before the people, they devised a scheme to shut him up for good. They bribed evil men to bring up false charges against him. The Jewish people, elders and scribes caught Stephen and brought him before the council. False witnesses accused him of blasphemy against the holy place and the Mosaic law.

For we have heard him say, that this Jesus of Nazareth shall destroy this place, and shall change the customs which Moses delivered us. And all that sat in the council, looking stedfastly on him, saw his face as it had been the face of an angel. (Acts 6:14-15)

Stephen had the confidence of one who had unchangeable faith in God. This gave him the appearance of calmness and serenity; his countenance was illuminated as the "face of an angel."

> And he said, Men, brethren, and fathers, hearken; The God of glory appeared unto our father Abraham, when he was in Mesopotamia, before he dwelt in Charran, (Acts 7:2)

Stephen's powerful defense of the Gospel was a summary of the history of the Jews, beginning with their father, Abraham, and his calling. He spoke of the Abrahamic Covenant, the Covenant of Circumcision, the journey into Egypt, the bondage that came upon them there, the deliverance provided through the leadership of Moses, the forty-year journey in the wilderness, and the temple of Solomon. Finally, he confronted them with their hypocrisy and sins.

> Which of the prophets have not your fathers persecuted? and they have slain them which shewed before of the coming of the Just One; of whom ye have been now the betrayers and murderers: Who have received the law by the disposition of angels, and have not kept it. (Acts 7:52-53)

This enraged the crowd to such an extent that they did not wait for the council to rend judgment. "When they heard these things, they were cut to the heart, and they gnashed on him with their teeth" (Acts 7:54).

Stephen did not focus on the crowd and their anger. He looked up and saw the glory of God and Jesus standing at his right side. He was stoned when he spoke of the vision.

Then they cried out with a loud voice, and stopped their ears, and ran upon him with one accord, And cast him out of the city, and stoned him: and the witnesses laid down their clothes at a young man's feet, whose name was Saul. (Acts 7:57-58)

Stephen underwent a painful persecution, death at the hands of a hysterical mob. Closely observing was a very young Saul, whom the people laid down their coats at his feet. Saul was consenting to the death of Stephen. He did not know it, but he would one day become tantamount in spreading the Gospel.

And they stoned Stephen, calling upon God, and saying, Lord Jesus, receive my spirit. And he kneeled down, and cried with a loud voice, Lord, lay not this sin to their charge. And when he had said this, he fell asleep. (Acts 7:59-60)

Stephen prayed for those who stoned him as Jesus had prayed for all mankind on the cross, that they would be forgiven. At the violent death of Stephen, the Jewish leaders were emboldened to take sternly repressive measures to crush the new movement. The majority of the Christians in Jerusalem were scattered abroad throughout Judea and Samaria by the persecution. The church in Jerusalem was strongly Judaistic in character, maintaining some observance of the law. The scattering, or dispersion, of its believers resulted in numerous missionary projects.

It is remarkable that it took persecution for the church to begin to take the Gospel into "Judaea, and in Samaria, and unto the uttermost part of the earth" (Acts 1:8b).

Sometimes our suffering is a pivotal force that becomes our testimony to the world. Stephen's suffering pivoted him from earth to glory. He was a force to be reckoned with, a formidable man.

32 PHILIP

And the saying pleased the whole multitude: and they chose Stephen, a man full of faith and of the Holy Ghost, and Philip, and Prochorus, and Nicanor, and Timon, and Parmenas, and Nicolas a proselyte of Antioch. (Acts 6:5)

Philip was one of the seven men appointed to the care of the widows of the Jerusalem church. Severe persecution of the church burst upon it very suddenly, beginning with the death of Stephen. Saul, who not only witnessed the stoning of Stephen but the coats of those stoning him were laid at his feet, made it dangerous to remain in one place. He harassed the Christian community, entering every house, dragging out both men and women and committing them to prison. But for the intervention of almighty God, the church would certainly have been brought to a screeching halt.

> Therefore they that were scattered abroad went every where preaching the word. Then Philip went down to the city of Samaria, and preached Christ unto them. And the people with one accord gave

heed unto those things which Philip spake, hearing and seeing the miracles which he did. For unclean spirits, crying with loud voice, came out of many that were possessed with them: and many taken with palsies, and that were lame, were healed. (Acts 8:4-7)

The seven men appointed to care for the Jerusalem church widows were not content to remain servers of tables. Two of them are mentioned as preachers. Stephen became an apologist and the first martyr. Philip became an evangelist. Driven from Jerusalem by the tumult of the persecution, Philip made his way to Samaria, where he preached Christ and demonstrated the power of the Holy Ghost through miracles and words.

The Samaritans were half Gentile. They adhered to Yahvey (or Yahweh) but retained some of the heathen features of the Assyrians who conquered the northern kingdom in 721 B.C. There was much tension between the Samaritans and the Jews, who did not regard them as true Jews. Therefore, the preaching of Philip in Samaria was a surprising action for a Jew. His preaching was met with an amazing response from the Samaritans. They forsook their superstitions and believed in Christ.

There was beforehand in Samaria a sorcerer named Simon, who bewitched the people and had a great name among them. But when they believed Philip, they repented and were baptized.

Then Simon himself believed also: and when he was baptized, he continued with Philip, and wondered, beholding the miracles and signs which were done. (Acts 8:13)

When Simon heard the preaching of Philip and saw the miracles and signs done at his hand, he believed and was also baptized.

When the apostles at Jerusalem heard of Philip's work in Samaria, they sent Peter and John, who prayed they might receive the Holy Ghost. They laid hands upon the people, and they received the Holy Ghost.

Simon, seeing the power of the Holy Ghost on the people, offered Peter and John money to give him the secret of the power. He was strongly rebuked and told to repent. "Then answered Simon, and said, Pray ye to the Lord for me, that none of these things which ye have spoken come upon me" (Acts 8:24).

An angel of the Lord spoke to Philip, telling him to arise and go down from Jerusalem to Gaza, a desert place.

And he arose and went: and, behold, a man of Ethiopia, an eunuch of great authority under Candace queen of the Ethiopians, who had the charge of all her treasure, and had come to Jerusalem for to worship, was returning, and sitting in his chariot read Esaias the prophet. (Acts 8:27-28)

The Spirit told Philip to go up to the man's chariot. Philip asked the man if he understood what he was reading. The man said he could not understand it without someone explaining the meaning. He asked Philip to come up into his chariot and speak with him.

> The place of the scripture which he read was this, He was led as a sheep to the slaughter; and like a lamb dumb before his shearer, so opened he not his mouth: In his humiliation his judgment was taken away: and who shall declare his generation? for his life is taken from the earth. (Acts 8:32-33)

The eunuch asked Philip if Isaiah was speaking about himself or some other prophet. Philip did a strange thing. He preached an entire sermon to just one individual, and that individual an Ethiopian in the court of Queen Candace. "Then Philip opened his mouth, and began at the same scripture, and preached unto him Jesus" (Acts 8:35). The eunuch believed, and when they came to a place where there was water, asked if he could be baptized.

> And Philip said, If thou believest with all thine heart, thou mayest. And he answered and said, I believe that Jesus Christ is the Son of God. And he commanded the chariot to stand still: and they went down both into the water, both Philip and the eunuch; and he baptized him. (Acts 8:37-38)

Philip's witness and sermon to the Ethiopian eunuch was further proof that the Gospel overcame racial backgrounds and prejudices. It demonstrated the method of preaching Jesus from the Old Testament and showed that the ministry to an individual was as important in the eyes of God as a mass revival. The eunuch was saved and baptized.

And when they were come up out of the water, the Spirit of the Lord caught away Philip, that the eunuch saw him no more: and he went on his way rejoicing. But Philip was found at Azotus: and passing through he preached in all the cities, till he came to Caesarea. (Acts 8:39-40)

Philip was caught away by the power of the Lord. The eunuch saw him no more, but he had received the Lord and now had a sure foundation. Philip, meanwhile, went from city to city preaching in the name of Jesus. Philip is last spoken of in the Bible in relation to Paul, who stayed at his home during one of his journeys.

And the next day we that were of Paul's company departed, and came unto Caesarea: and we entered into the house of Philip the evangelist, which was one of the seven; and abode with him. And the same man had four daughters, virgins, which did prophesy. (Acts 21:8-9)

We see that Philip was a great evangelist and had four daughters, who were also powerful in ministry. He brought up his children in the faith, and they, like their father, were advancing the Kingdom. Philip was a force to be reckoned with, a formidable man.

33 PAUL

Paul, an apostle, (not of men, neither by man, but by Jesus Christ, and God the Father, who raised him from the dead). (Galatians 1:1)

Paul clearly states his claim to apostleship. He was not an apostle because lots were cast to determine his worthiness. He was an apostle because he had a personal encounter with the Savior and was called and set into that position.

Paul is also called Saul. Saul was his Hebrew name, and Paul was his Roman name. Paul is the Latinized version of Saul. Both names are used interchangeably. He was the same Saul, who stood by consenting to the stoning of Stephen, the first martyr for the Christian faith, "and the witnesses laid down their clothes at a young man's feet, whose name was Saul" (Acts 7:58).

And Saul was consenting unto his death. And at that time there was a great persecution against the church which was at Jerusalem; and they were all scattered abroad throughout the regions of Judaea and Samaria, except the apostles. (Acts 8:1)

Paul had been an instigator and active participant in the sudden, severe persecution thrust upon the church, beginning with the death of Stephen. But that persecution was also the means of dispersing witnesses of the gospel throughout the regions of Judaea and Samaria.

As for Saul, he made havock of the church, entering into every house, and haling men and women committed them to prison. Therefore they that were scattered abroad went every where preaching the word. (Acts 8:3-4)

But for the intervention of almighty God, the church would certainly have been brought to a screeching halt by the efforts of one man.

And Saul, yet breathing out threatenings and slaughter against the disciples of the Lord, went unto the high priest, And desired of him letters to Damascus to the synagogues, that if he found any of this way, whether they were men or women, he might bring them bound unto Jerusalem. (Acts 9:1-2)

It was a usual day for the zealous young Paul. He went to the high priest and asked for letters to go to synagogues in Damascus and, if he found any Christians there, to arrest them and bring them to Jerusalem to be imprisoned. He was determined to squelch the Jesus movement by any means necessary. But on this day, Paul had an unexpected encounter with a force he could not reckon with.

"And as he journeyed, he came near Damascus: and suddenly there shined round about him a light from heaven" (Acts 9:3). The light shined around Paul brighter than the noonday sun, blinding him. He and his company fell to the ground.

> And when we were all fallen to the earth, I heard a voice speaking unto me, and saying in the Hebrew tongue, Saul, Saul, why persecutest thou me? it is hard for thee to kick against the pricks. (Acts 26:14)

A voice spoke to Paul in the Hebrew language. Paul asked, "Who art thou?" The heavenly voice said, "I am Jesus whom thou persecutest" (Acts 26:15).

Blinded by the brilliance of the light, trembling, and astonished, Paul asked what the Lord would have him do (Acts 9:6). He received his great commission.

> But rise, and stand upon thy feet: for I have appeared unto thee for this purpose, to make thee a minister and a witness both of these things which thou hast seen, and of those things in the which I will appear unto thee; Delivering thee from the people, and from the Gentiles, unto whom now I send thee, To open their eyes, and to turn them from darkness to light, and from the power of Satan unto God, that they may receive forgiveness of sins, and inheritance among them which are sanctified by faith that is in me. (Acts 26:16-18)

Paul was to continue the journey to Damascus, and he would be told what he must do there. The men with him heard the voice but did not see anyone. They led a blind

Paul into the city. Paul was still going to Damascus, but his plans were divinely changed, and so was his entire life. He had been arrested by the Holy Spirit. Know that in your journey, you may run from your assignment, but God will arrest you. Paul was in Damascus for three days and nights without eating or drinking.

The Lord appeared to Ananias, a disciple in the city, and sent him to Paul. He told him that Paul had seen him in a vision, putting his hand on him so that he might receive his sight. Paul's reputation and acts preceded him. He was a menace to the society of those who believed in Christ. Ananias was hesitant because Paul had heavily persecuted the church and had papers from the chief priest to arrest anyone calling on the name of Jesus.

But the Lord said unto him, Go thy way: for he is a chosen vessel unto me, to bear my name before the Gentiles, and kings, and the children of Israel: For I will shew him how great things he must suffer for my name's sake. (Acts 9:15-16)

Ananias obeyed the command. He entered the house where Paul was staying and told him he was sent so he might receive his sight and the Holy Ghost.

And immediately there fell from his eyes as it had been scales: and he received sight forthwith, and arose, and was baptized. And when he had received meat, he was strengthened. Then was Saul certain days with the disciples which were at Damascus. And straightway he preached Christ in the synagogues, that he is the Son of God. (Acts 9:18-20)

Paul traveled a short distance away into Arabia for a short time after his conversion, then returned to Damascus where he lived for three years before going to Jerusalem.

> But when it pleased God, who separated me from my mother's womb, and called me by his grace, To reveal his Son in me, that I might preach him among the heathen; immediately I conferred not with flesh and blood: Neither went I up to Jerusalem to them which were apostles before me; but I went into Arabia, and returned again unto Damascus. Then after three years I went up to Jerusalem to see Peter, and abode with him fifteen days. But other of the apostles saw I none, save James the Lord's brother. (Galatians 1:15-19)

Paul's conversion was supernatural in nature. The appearance of Jesus at his conversion is confirmation of his apostolic status. He was chosen to be the apostle to the Gentiles.

Paul's conversion is perhaps the most important event in the history of Christianity, next to the work of Christ Himself. It not only removed "public enemy number one" but transformed him into one of the chief defenders of the gospel. While the ministry of Philip illustrated the church's outreach to new localities and groups, the conversion of Saul of Tarsus provided a new leader.

> Circumcised the eighth day, of the stock of Israel, of the tribe of Benjamin, an Hebrew of the Hebrews; as touching the law, a Pharisee; Concerning zeal, persecuting the church; touching the righteousness which is in the law, blameless. (Philippians 3:5-6)

The converted Paul put his whole confidence in Christ. He gladly suffered persecution and troubles to tell the world that the Messiah had come. Paul had much that he could have boasted of in the flesh. He could have boasted that he was brought up at the feet of Gamaliel, one of the foremost Hebrew scholars of his day (Acts 22:3); he could have made his boast in his knowledge of the law, in his former position on the Sanhedrin council, and in his impeccable background as "an Hebrew of the Hebrews" (Philippians 3:1-7).

Paul was born to strict Hebrew parents of the tribe of Benjamin in Tarsus, a city in the busy metropolis of Cilicia. He was a Roman citizen by birth (Acts 22:28). He was a Pharisee and perhaps a member of the Sanhedrin. By the Mosaic law, he was blameless. None of these things were important to Paul. He counted their loss as nothing for having gained the "excellency of the knowledge of Christ Jesus" (Philippians 3:8.).

The gospel message began to expand, and the purpose of God in reaching the Gentiles became increasingly evident. The center of the message shifted from the restoration of the kingdom to the forgiveness of sins. The inclusion of the Gentiles precipitated questions involving the interpretation of the law as it should – or should not – be applied to the Gentiles.

The mother of all the Gentile churches was the church of Antioch in Syria, founded as part of the sudden expansion that came in the period of transition. With the establishment of the church of Antioch, the missionary movement to the Gentiles began. The disciples were called

Christians first in Antioch (Acts 11:2). It was at Antioch where the first controversy over the status of Gentiles began. It was also the center where the leaders of the church met.

By 46 A.D., the church of Antioch was well established. Their missionary achievements included sponsoring a relief expedition to Jerusalem to carry a contribution to those who were suffering because of famine. While they were engaged in the course of regular worship and fasting, "the Holy Ghost said, Separate me Barnabas and Saul for the work whereunto I have called them" (Acts 13:2). They obeyed the direction of the Holy Spirit, consecrating Barnabas and Paul for the special service of the Lord and sending them on their mission.

Their first gospel campaign was conducted in Cyprus. In the conflict with Elymas, the sorcerer, Paul, came to the fore by rebuking him publicly and pronouncing judgment on him. The swift retribution amazed the proconsul, and he "believed" (Acts 13:12). Mark also accompanied Barnabas and Paul on their first missionary journey as an assistant (Acts 12:25). However, he returned to Jerusalem before they completed their mission (Acts 13:13).

We must note the change in leadership that occurs in Cyprus. In Acts 13:2, the team is described as "Barnabas and Saul," giving Barnabas the place of prominence as the senior missionary and calling Paul by his Jewish name. In Acts 13:9, Saul is called "Paul," and thereafter, he is referred to by the name the world has come to know. In Acts 13:13, the team is described as "Paul and his company," using Paul's Gentile name. Thereafter, Paul is in the place of prominence. The event in Cyprus brought out his leadership qualifications and placed him in undisputed command of the mission.

At Antioch of Pisidia, Paul introduced a new and bold advance in the truth concerning Jesus Christ: Justification individually before God solely on the ground of faith. The outcome of Paul's teaching was twofold. It was met with bitter opposition from the Jews (13:45). Paul then announced that he would "turn to the Gentiles" (13:46). As a result, the Gentiles became the core of the new church in Antioch of Pisidia.

The question as to what extent the Gentiles should be required to observe the precepts of the law became such a source of contention in the church that Paul, Barnabas, and some others went to Jerusalem to discuss the matter with the apostles and elders (Acts 15:1-29). A council was held. The decision of the council that the Gentiles not be required to keep all the law but abstain from certain practices was put into writing. Delegates were sent to Antioch, with Paul and Barnabas bearing the written record of the proceedings.

And they wrote letters by them after this manner; The apostles and elders and brethren send greeting unto the brethren which are of the Gentiles in Antioch and Syria and Cilicia: Forasmuch as we have heard, that certain which went out from us have troubled you with words, subverting your souls, saying, Ye must be circumcised, and keep the law: to whom we gave no such commandment: It seemed good unto us, being assembled with one accord, to send chosen men unto you with our beloved Barnabas and Paul, Men that have hazarded their lives for the name of our Lord Jesus Christ. We have sent therefore Judas and Silas, who shall also tell you the same things by mouth. (Acts 15:23-27)

These and similar problems were reflected in many books of the New Testament written between 50 A.D. and 60 A.D. Two of these dealt so specifically with this subject that they have been called the "literature of protest." The Epistle of James insists that faith produces works. Paul's epistle to the Galatians stresses religious freedom. Both recognized the need for transformation of the individual by the grace of God.

Paul and his company returned to Antioch after the close of the council of Jerusalem, where he and Barnabas spent some time teaching and preaching. Paul proposed that they visit the churches they had planted as a follow-up and to confirm them in the faith. It is the mark of a good shepherd to care for the flock entrusted to him, and have concern for their spiritual growth.

And Barnabas determined to take with them John, whose surname was Mark. But Paul thought not good to take him with them, who departed from them from Pamphylia, and went not with them to the work. And the contention was so sharp between them, that they departed asunder one from the other: and so Barnabas took Mark, and sailed unto Cyprus; And Paul chose Silas, and departed, being recommended by the brethren unto the grace of God. And he went through Syria and Cilicia, confirming the churches. (Acts 15:37-41)

Barnabas wanted to take John Mark with them. Paul disagreed because John Mark had returned home before the first missionary journey was completed. The situation was resolved by Barnabas taking John Mark with him to Cyprus and Paul choosing Silas, a delegate to Antioch from the Jerusalem council, to travel with him north through Syria and Cilicia toward the frontiers of Asia Minor. During this journey, Paul found Timothy and added him to his company. Timothy was a young convert whose mother was a Jewess and whose father was Greek.

Paul had a vision of a Macedonian man beseeching him to "Come over into Macedonia, and help us" (Acts16:9). He immediately accepted the Macedonian call, and the evangelism of Europe and all of the effect of the gospel on Western civilization began.

In Philippi, Paul was led of the spirit to cast out a demon from a slave girl, a clairvoyant who had been a source of wealth to her masters during his ministry in the city. Enraged at the loss of their business, they brought false charges against Paul and Silas, accusing them of teaching unlawful customs (Acts 16:21). Paul and Silas were imprisoned and beaten. "And at midnight Paul and Silas prayed, and sang praises unto God: and the prisoners heard them" (Acts 16:25). An earthquake shook the prison. The jailer was saved by this event and released them.

In Thessalonica, some of the Jews believed, and there was a great response among the Greeks. Among those who disagreed arose an opposition that became so intense that the evangelists fled the city by night to Berea, where their message was met with greater success until a delegation from Thessalonica descended upon them and attacked Paul. Silas and Timothy remained behind in Berea for awhile to complete the work, and the church flourished.

Paul traveled to Corinth, where the Temple of Aphrodite lodged at one time one thousand priestesses who were professional prostitutes and where the vilest kind of life could be found. Paul was reunited with Silas and Timothy at Corinth.

From Corinth, Paul wrote to the church in Thessalonica. In his first letter to the Thessalonians, he praises them for their steadfastness under persecution by the Jews and corrected certain errors and misunderstandings that had grown up among them. The Thessalonian epistles contain the earliest full discussion concerning the return of Christ. In I Thessalonians, he also addresses sexual immorality. In the second epistle to the Thessalonians, Paul removes the misapprehension that "the day of Christ is at hand" (2 Thessalonians 2:2). In these two epistles, almost every major doctrine of the Christian faith is represented.

Paul left Corinth in the company of Aquila and Priscilla, stopping in Ephesus, where Aquila and Priscilla set up headquarters and began their ministry. In his first letter to the Corinthians, Paul deals with doctrinal matters. In the second letter, he deals with personal matters.

Returning to Ephesus, Paul began his mission in Asia. Paul faced several important problems in Ephesus. Among them was whether the baptism of John was sufficient to produce a full Christian experience. Another problem of the Asian mission was the occult.

Paul planned to visit Rome in the next step of his missionary journey and wrote the Epistle to the Romans in preparation. The letter to the church at Rome was written from Corinth about 57 A.D. or 58 A.D. during Paul's third missionary journey. Paul had not yet been to Rome, but he stated his desire to visit them (Romans 1:10). In his introduction, he calls himself "a servant of Jesus Christ" (Romans 1:1). The Greek word translated here as servant is "doulos." It means bond-servant or slave and carries the connotation of one who voluntarily gives themselves to the control of another. It implies one who has subjugated his will to do the will of another.

While Romans is not a complete summary of Paul's theology, several major doctrinal truths are presented in the letter, covering a series of theological themes that include the plan of salvation, the righteousness of God revealed, and justification by faith. While these are all of critical importance in the letter, the overall theme of Romans is the gospel. The gospel is the saving power of God for everyone who believes, and the gospel makes known God's righteousness by faith.

Paul referred to the special favor God conferred upon him by his apostolic calling and divinely appointed commission. This obligated him to preach the gospel to everyone possible. He says, "I am debtor both to the Greeks, and to the Barbarians; both to the wise, and to the unwise" (Romans 1:14). The Greek word *barbarous* refers to anyone who is a non-Greek. Paul is including all nations and classes of people as those to whom he is under divine obligation to preach to. Paul fully recognized he had a responsibility to preach the whole counsel of God to the whole world; he was eager to proclaim the good news of Jesus Christ in the imperial city of Rome as he had done in other places, and he was not afraid of the consequences which might be a result of proclaiming such a bold message (Romans 1:14-16).

The gospel is not about a man, it's not about you, and it's not about me. It's about Jesus Christ and him, God incarnate. He is the content of the gospel. The gospel is what has the power to unleash the work of God unto salvation in a person, whether that person is Jew or Gentile.

The Jews were a special people entrusted with a special privilege in the outworking of God's plan. They were the instruments God used to bring a blessing to all people. However, the Great Commission did not distinguish between Jews and Gentiles. It was for "all nations" (Matthew 28:19). To the Jews who despised and rejected the gospel, it became a stumbling block; to the Greeks, it was mere foolishness (1 Corinthians 1:23); but to those who believe in Christ, it is able to deliver completely from every devastating ruin of sin; from "corruptible to incorruptible" (1 Peter 1:23).

The last section of Acts tells us of Paul's imprisonment, trials, and voyage to Rome. It seemingly has no conclusion but ends with Paul imprisoned. It gives us insight into the inner thought and teaching of Paul more than the other passages in Acts.

Paul undertook the financial responsibility of helping some Jewish Christians to discharge the Nazarite vow

(Acts 21:23-24). The Jews from Asia caused a riot of such proportions that the Roman military tribune had to intervene. Gaining permission from the tribune to speak from the castle steps, Paul addressed the crowd in Hebrew, making his defense.

The crowd listened respectfully until Paul mentioned the call to the Gentiles. Paul was removed from the castle for safety. He was placed in protective custody for four years. He stayed in Caesarea for two years until he appealed to Caesar and was sent to Rome, where waiting for the hearing consumed another two years.

During his imprisonment, Paul continued to teach and write. In Rome, he dwelt in his own hired house, where he carried on a ministry to all who called on him there (Acts 28:30-31). The four epistles known as the Prison Epistles, Philippians, Colossians, Ephesians, and Philemon were written during this time. As a group, they deal with general teaching.

Philemon was written at the same time as Ephesians and Colossians. Onesimus, a slave, had run away from his owner, Philemon, taking with him some of his master's property. He met Paul and was converted. Paul sent him back to make right the wrong he had done with a note requesting that he be received and forgiven.

Ephesians is the one writing in the New Testament in which the word "church" means the church universal rather than the local group. It informs the Gentiles of their new calling and discloses the mystery of the body of Christ in which there is neither Jew nor Gentile, bond or free. It is not written to novices but to those who have achieved some measure of spiritual maturity and wish to gain fuller knowledge. Its goal is "the unity of the faith . . . the knowledge of the Son of God . . . the measure of the stature of the fullness of Christ" (Ephesians 4:13).

Colossians bears a close resemblance to Ephesians. Paul himself had probably not visited Colosse. He was moved to write as an antidote to a blasé intellectualism infecting Colosse, promoting a false philosophy of mysteries, secret knowledge, and wisdom while discounting Christ.

Philippians is the most personal of all the epistles of Paul that were not written to individuals. Because of their intense loyalty to Paul, he felt that he could speak to them freely of his tribulations and spiritual ambitions. Two main topics dominate the Epistle to the Philippians: One is the gospel, and the other is joy. Philippians is a note of thanks for gifts received and an expression of Paul's personal Christian life.

In Philippians 3:12-14 one hears Paul bearing his very soul to us and the very essence of his life work when he says, ". . . forgetting those things which are behind, and reaching forth unto those things which are before, I press toward the mark for the prize of the high calling of God in Christ Jesus." Imprisoned, he speaks without bonds to let us know that the struggles he has faced are nothing compared to the prize that awaits him.

The Christian life is a walk of faith. In the Old Testament, faith looked towards the cross. In the New Testament, faith is looking back on the finished work of

Christ at the cross and toward his return. In both the Old and New Testaments, faith is a key element. Faith is only as valid as its object, and Christ is the object of the Christian faith. Implicit faith must be based on facts, or it is merely blind faith and blind faith cannot be substantiated. The Christian faith is based on the death, burial, and resurrection of Jesus Christ. It is a faith confirmed by facts, and the facts show that the gospel has the power to save everyone that believes because it is the revelation of the righteousness of God.

The Pastoral Epistles are I Timothy, Titus, and II Timothy. The biographical data that they supply indicates that Paul must have been acquitted on his first hearing before the emperor and that he enjoyed a free period of ministry thereafter.

There was some lapse of time within the range of the Pastoral Epistles. I Timothy pictures Paul as traveling and active, advising this young pastor concerning his duties. Titus is similar in outlook to I Timothy. II Timothy is a terminus, for Paul evidently was confident he would not survive the winter (II Timothy 4:21).

The first epistle to Timothy was written to instruct, encourage, and strengthen this young preacher for the tremendous task of pastoring the church at Ephesus, which Paul had assigned him to. He cautioned Timothy against the influence of false teachers (I Timothy 1:3-4).

Titus followed I Timothy in order of time. Paul had left Titus in Crete to complete the establishment of the church and to rectify its errors. The problems in Crete included disorganization and members who exhibited careless behavior. The general content of Titus is like that of I Timothy, except for a stronger emphasis on major doctrines of the church as it emerged into the institutional stage.

As mentioned, II Timothy is a terminus, a finishing point. It has an urgent tone as if Paul was arrested suddenly and sent back to Rome, and now, knowing that his time is short, must give final instructions. He asks that Timothy do his best to come see him before winter but writes in a manner that he realizes he may not make it before Paul is moved from the scene. He seems to be delegating his responsibilities to the younger generation of teachers who would be left to execute them.

I and II Timothy remind us of the great farewell speeches in the Old Testament: Jacob's blessings to his sons, Moses' farewell to the children of Israel, and, of course, Joshua's farewell to Israel. You can almost hear Paul saying that he has done everything that was charged to him, and he charges these young warriors with the same serious charge. His time on earth is fast coming to an end. He has used every minute of it in running the race well. He now looks forward to ". . . a crown of righteousness . . ." (II Timothy 4:8). At the same time, he is concerned that the work he established for the Lord continues and grows. It is full of personal sentiments, administrative policy, remembrances, instruction, and confidence that the work will continue. Though a certain sadness runs through it, it is full of hope. As in I Timothy, its main purpose is to strengthen Timothy for the task Paul is about to relinquish, a monumental challenge.

We must mention the charge Paul makes to Timothy. It is the charge given at every ordination service. "I charge thee therefore before God, and the Lord Jesus Christ, who shall judge the quick and the dead at his appearing and his kingdom; Preach the word; be instant in season, out of season; reprove, rebuke, exhort with all longsuffering and doctrine" (2 Timothy 4:1-2). It was the charge for the time then; it is the charge for the time now. It is for all ministers at all times in all places. The power of the charge resonates from a prison room down through the halls of history.

Paul kept the charge laid upon him. He could truly say, "I have fought a good fight, I have finished my course, I have kept the faith: Henceforth there is laid up for me a crown of righteousness, which the Lord, the righteous judge, shall give me at that day: and not to me only, but unto all them also that love his appearing" (2 Timothy 4:7-8).

Paul, the great apostle to the Gentiles, the great scholar of Mosaic Law, the great Hebrew of the Hebrews, the great chosen vessel, the great witness and minister of the gospel, the great prophet for his time, the great writer of most of the New Testament, one of the greatest warriors for Jesus Christ, was a force to be reckoned with, a formidable man.

ANONYMOUS

Understand that we cannot tell his entire story. There were things we learned after he was gone, and there are some things we will never know because he chose not to discuss them. Had he wanted you and I to know, he would have told us. He was my father; he was your father; he was our uncle; he was our brother; he was one of the deacons in the church; he was a teacher; he was that man who served as a hero, served as a mentor, showed great kindness and compassion. He may even be you.

His hands have been productive. He has worked to take care of the family. He has ministered to the poor and the sick. He has prayed for those who could not pray for themselves. He has taught other men and boys to be godly. He has advanced the Kingdom of God. He is a man among men.

His name is known to the countless number of people he has helped, even though there will never be a book written about him or a movie portraying his life. He is ever loved and appreciated by those whose lives he has impacted. This chapter is unnumbered because he is unnumbered. It is unrecognized because he will not recognize himself in it. He remains anonymous, a force to be reckoned with, a formidable man. Wherever this book is read in the whole world, let this that he has done be told for a memorial of him.

A FEW MORE FORMIDABLE MEN

This book would be incomplete if I did not acknowledge a few formidable men who have personally touched my life. My father, Henry Hampton, was a janitor who supported a wife and ten children on minimum wages. He lived to be 101.

My father had a cousin, Ira Ganyard, who lived with us and was a second father. He also taught in the church. He was a furniture upholsterer by trade. Ira had a beautiful voice and had a Christian group, "The Willing Travelers."

My mother's father, Willie Bennett I, was a preacher. He was our pastor in Louisiana, and when the family relocated to California. The deacons in the church were also teachers and mentors. The first chairman of Deacons in California was Earnest Humphrey, Sr., a mighty man of prayer and the patriarch of his family. My uncle, Nathaniel Strange, was superintendent of Sunday School. When he relocated to Texas, his brother, the faithful Spencer Strange, became the superintendent of Sunday School and later Chairman of Deacons.

I am deeply grateful to Tommy Redwood, another powerful man of prayer who served as Chairman of Deacons later.

I owe a great debt of gratitude to Roots Community Church, its pastoral staff, and some of its members for the many acts of kindness and Christian love you have shown toward my daughter. What you have done for her, you have done unto me. Thank you, Pastor Dylan Budd, Pastor Hans Anderle, and Pastor Alec Eisenberg. A special thank you to Mike Saia.

There have been many godly men who have had a major impact on my life. Among them are my fifth-grade teacher, Mr. Joshua, and a counselor at my high school, Mr. Madison. There are others. Please know that you are in my thoughts, and my gratitude goes out to each of you.

Formidable men marry formidable women, and I cannot thank any of these Christian warriors without acknowledging and thanking those women who march on the battlefield beside them.

Finally, let me thank Dr. Robert L. McKnight I, Pastor of Rock of Truth Baptist Church, one of the most formidable men I have ever met. Dr. McKnight is having a great walk. This phenomenal man was born to teach. He teaches from the pulpit and in the secular realm. Pastor McKnight served as the second chairperson of the African American Studies Department at Berkeley High School, the first ever African American Studies Department (AASD) in a public high school in the United States. After retirement, he served as an adjunct professor of African

American Studies at the college level for years. He taught African Civilization, African American History, Social Psychology of Black Male/Female Relationships, The Black Family, Religion and The Black Church, Roots of African American Culture, Introduction of African American Studies, and African Psychology.

Dr. McKnight believes in a strong family. He has an equally accomplished wife and four outstanding children.

I have never heard Dr. McKnight say anything negative or disparaging of anyone. He feels every man has potential, has redemptive value, and deserves a chance. He is a spiritual optimist. With him, the cup is not just half full; it is brimming over. You can't sit under his teaching and remain negative, critical, or despondent. Dr. McKnight says that when you are at your lowest, when you have nothing at all, that is the best time to attempt great things. I immediately understood this profound truth with my mind when I heard it, but it was some time before my spirit encapsulated it. I am grateful for the inspiration. "For with God nothing shall be impossible" (Luke 1:37).

Dr. McKnight believes in passing the mantle and in mentoring others. Serving under him are men of the same caliber. Two young ministers faithfully uphold his hands in ministry: Minister Joseph Lynch and Minister Larry Johnson II. The lead Deacon is the faithful Otis Todd. Assisting in the diaconate is my brother, another prayer warrior, Tommy Hampton.

I praise God for all of these men among men. They are forces to be reckoned with, formidable men.

Made in the USA
Monee, IL
31 May 2024

59165124R10133